HAND
MADE
HOME

MARK & SALLY BAILEY

PHOTOGRAPHY BY DEBI TRELOAR

HAND
MADE
HOME

RYLAND
PETERS
& SMALL

LONDON NEW YORK

SENIOR DESIGNER
Megan Smith

COMMISSIONING EDITOR
Annabel Morgan

LOCATION RESEARCH
Jess Walton

PRODUCTION CONTROLLER
Toby Marshall

ART DIRECTOR
Leslie Harrington

PUBLISHING DIRECTOR
Alison Starling

STYLING Mark Bailey

First published in 2011
by Ryland Peters & Small
20–21 Jockey's Fields
London WC1R 4BW
and
519 Broadway, 5th Floor
New York, NY 10012
www.rylandpeters.com

Text copyright
© Mark and Sally Bailey 2011
Design and photographs
copyright
© Ryland Peters & Small 2011

10 9 8 7 6 5 4 3 2
ISBN 978-1-84975-155-1

A CIP record for this book
is available from the British
Library.

Printed and bound in China

Library of Congress CIP data
has been applied for.

CONTENTS

THE
INTRODUCTION

THE INSPIRATION FOR THIS BOOK CAME FROM A RECENT, LONG-AWAITED TRIP TO KETTLE'S YARD IN CAMBRIDGE, ENGLAND – A BEAUTIFUL AND INSPIRING HOUSE THAT ALSO HAPPENS TO BE HOME TO A MODERN ART GALLERY. KETTLE'S YARD STARTED LIFE AS FOUR ALMOST DERELICT COTTAGES. JIM EDE, A FORMER CURATOR AT THE TATE GALLERY LONDON, RESTORED AND REMODELLED THEM INTO A HOME THAT WAS INTENDED NOT ONLY AS A PLACE TO LIVE, BUT ALSO A SPACE IN WHICH ART COULD BE ENJOYED AND WHERE EDE COULD SHARE THE COLLECTION OF ART AND OBJECTS THAT HE HAD AMASSED OVER FIFTY YEARS.

Kettle's Yard is a place we've been aiming to visit for many years, but what finally spurred us on to make the trip was our recent purchase of a house/gallery (see pages 78–87) near Hay-on-Wye in rural Herefordshire. Our plan is to use this house in a similar way – as a gallery space that's home to a collection of art and our favourite handmade objects, but also as a comfortable home and retreat that we can escape to when we want to get away from our busy Baileys home store near Ross-on-Wye.

Living with painting, sculpture, ceramics and handmade textiles in a domestic setting is a very different experience to viewing these pieces in an art gallery, many of which resemble white cubes that can feel rather sterile or soulless. Not many people would choose to live in such surroundings. The handmade home is all about creating an integrated space where you can live alongside the pieces that make up and define you and your family's tastes as they develop over time, pieces that will become part of the fabric of your home.

When it comes to living with handmade pieces, a sense of balance is essential – you don't want to end up with a house that's bursting at the seams with wonderful things that can't be seen properly because they are overwhelmed by one other. The handmade home should be filled with favourite treasures displayed in a way that's well-considered and frequently edited, allowing the objects to be appreciated and enjoyed and lending your home a contemporary feel and a calm, almost serene atmosphere where everything coexists in harmony (for most of the time, at least!).

The book opens by considering ways in which you can begin to introduce the handmade into your home, and suggesting how to create the ideal background for your treasures. The second half of the book visits the homes of a clutch of designers, makers and artists who kindly allowed us to visit and photograph their own private spaces, where they live with handmade objects easily and beautifully on a daily basis.

OUR PHILOSOPHY

WE BELIEVE THAT YOUR HOME SHOULD BE A
PLACE WHERE YOU CAN LET YOUR CREATIVE
SIDE LOOSE – SOMEWHERE TO DISPLAY YOUR
FAVOURITE THINGS, WHERE HANDMADE PIECES
AND OTHER TREASURES SIT HARMONIOUSLY
ALONGSIDE THE FURNITURE, FIXTURES AND
FITTINGS AS WELL AS ALL THE OTHER EVERYDAY
STUFF WE NEED IN ORDER TO GET THROUGH
THE WEEK. WITH CAREFUL CONSIDERATION
AND ATTENTION TO DETAIL, YOUR HOME CAN
BECOME A WORK OF ART IN ITS OWN RIGHT.

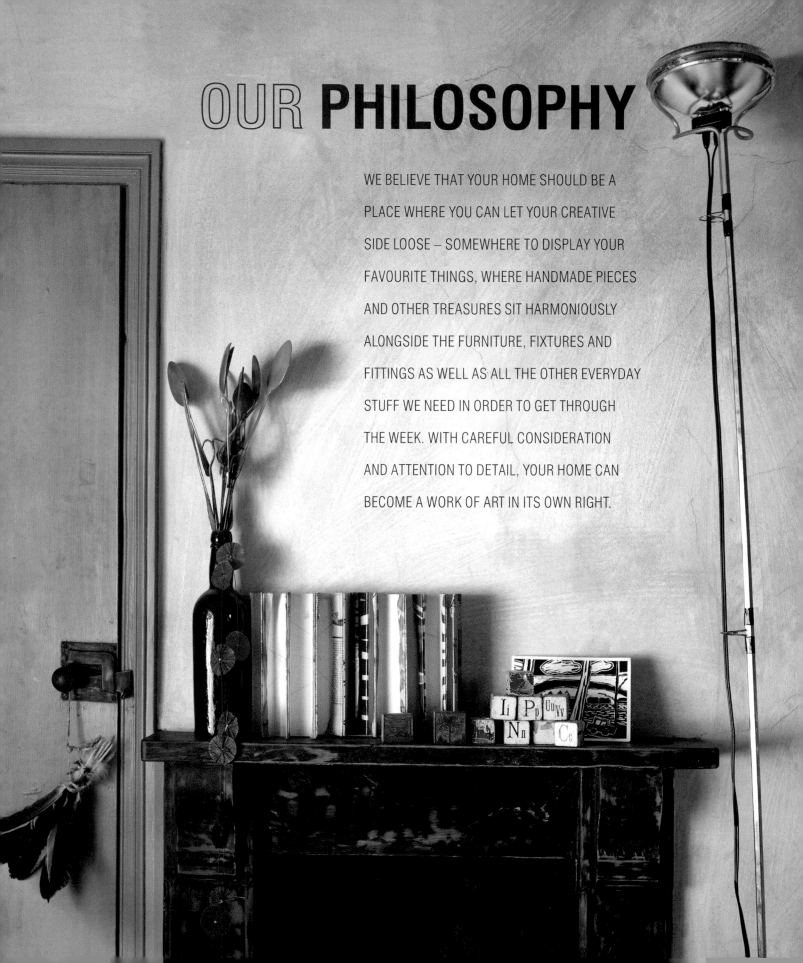

If this sounds too much like hard work, please don't be put off – it's not! The handmade home makes a virtue out of imperfection. The odd splash of paint here and uneven edges there all add to the relaxed atmosphere, so there's no need to be precious. Perfection is not required, nor even sought after. Instead, create a home that celebrates the handmade in all its irregular, unique beauty.

Initially the main consideration – where the 'hard work' comes in – is how to build up a collection of the handmade. Prints, paintings, ceramics and sculpture all tend to be the domain of

RIGHT AND BELOW Leslie Oschmann, former visual director of Anthropologie, collects old oil paintings from Dutch flea markets and reworks them as chair covers, bags and other objects. They fill her home, which doubles as her studio. Canvases awaiting transformation are hung together, creating a new conversation between the subjects of the paintings.

art galleries, which can seem rather off-putting and intimidating at first. However, once you've dipped your toes in a couple of times, you will grow in confidence and be well on the way to realizing exactly what it is that you like. And this is the really important bit, because any collection of art or craft – whether it includes fine art or a set of handcrafted wooden spoons – should be made up of pieces that you feel passionate about, not things that someone else has told you that you should like. Be true to your tastes and confident in your decision-making, and you will stay on the right track.

The handmade home encompasses much more than collections of fine art. If you are unsure of exactly where to start, small steps such as choosing handcrafted plates or drinking your morning coffee from a hand-thrown mug are the right way to begin. You'll soon become aware that using items made by

OPPOSITE A collection of handmade art objects are displayed on a dark painted mantelpiece. They include a 'bouquet' of twisted cutlery/flatware, a concertina book and a pile of vintage alphabet blocks.

OPPOSITE Our informal dining space is filled with an array of handmade objects that sit comfortably together thanks to their similar tones, which echo the colours of the whole room. An Afghan bowl sits on the curve-fronted pine cupboard alongside a ceramic vessel by Dylan Bowen. A primitive-looking oil by David Pearce rests against the wall, framing the ceramic collection. A further group of stoneware jugs from Dijon sit on a pre-cast concrete shelf. The folding trestle table surrounded by French steel stacking chairs lends the room an informal air of village hall chic.

ABOVE It is important to carefully consider how you arrange your collections, as the addition of one seemingly random object will often transform the grouping. On our kitchen shelf, an old tin truck has been parked next to a couple of robust-looking speckled jugs by studio potter Andrew Crouch and above stacks of wobbly plates and rows of hand-blown glasses.

hand makes for a much more pleasurable, tactile everyday experience; one that awakens your senses, reminds you of the natural world and opens your home up to all kinds of new possibilities.

Make it your mission to search out unusual pieces. Visit flea markets or antique fairs and rummage for salvaged treasures. Try to see the possibilities inherent in everything. Even old paintings can be made into something useful, if you take a leaf out of Leslie Oschmann's book. The former visual director of Anthropologie recycles old canvases bought at flea markets into bags and seat covers. Empty frames have their uses, too – simply prop them up against a white wall, layering a few to create a multi-dimensional display.

Old shop signs and fittings will bring a graphic element to an interior. Similarly, discarded industrial objects can be given a new home and a new purpose. When gathered together, the functionality and simplicity of their design takes centre stage and

is further enhanced when juxtaposed with beautiful works of art or placed alongside a delicate piece of porcelain or glassware. The same goes for found objects too, by which we mean things you've picked up on walks in the country or on the beach on holiday. Seemingly mundane items such as a beautiful feather or a handful of pebbles can, if carefully and cleverly positioned, sit happily alongside more conventional art in your home.

Once your collection of handmade pieces starts to take shape, you will need to think about how best to group and display it. You'll find that you will experience a sudden flash of alchemy when you put two seemingly disparate objects next to each other then find a third item that provides a link in some way. Step back and take a moment to enjoy the subtle conversation that begins to take place.

Take the time to consider the backdrop to your handmade treasures. In order to keep the atmosphere harmonious, we suggest that you keep the bones of your home simple and quiet. Anything overly elaborate or decorative may distract from the handmade pieces, which should be the main focus. Keep walls neutral and, if you can, use natural materials underfoot, such as wooden boards or stone (after all, you can always keep your feet warm with a hand-woven rug or two).

THE
ELEMENTS

colour texture **textiles** made by hand **collecting & curating**

COLOUR

COLOUR CREEPS INTO THE HANDMADE
HOME IN ALL SORTS OF UNEXPECTED WAYS,
GIVING YOU THE FREEDOM TO LET COLOURS
CHOOSE THEMSELVES. THE OBJECTS YOU
SURROUND YOURSELF WITH WILL PROVIDE
THE STARTING POINT FOR YOUR COLOUR
SCHEME, AND FINDING OTHER THINGS TO
SIT WITH THEM IS WHERE THE REAL FUN
BEGINS. IN THE MEANTIME, ALL YOU ARE
EXPECTED TO DO IS TO PROVIDE THE MORE
FLAMBOYANT COLOURS IN YOUR ART AND
CRAFT COLLECTION WITH A GENTLE,
CALMING BACKDROP.

PREVIOUS PAGE Painting by William Brown.
LEFT Balls of dark paper string from Nepal show how even a flash of colour, here in the form of the blue twine used to bind the string in place, is enough to awaken the senses.
RIGHT A pile of vintage linens provides a resting place for a string of beads.

The starting point for decorating your home usually involves shuffling through piles of paint charts followed by endless wanderings up and down the aisles of your local DIY store as you try to decide on the colour scheme you want to live with. But the handmade home dictates a slightly different decorating journey, so stop and take a step or two back before you dive into the nearest paint pot.

Our philosophy is to think of the walls as a blank canvas or backdrop that will allow your favourite things to speak for themselves. You may find that a paint colour that looks fabulous in the tin may grab the limelight or jar with your handmade pieces once on the wall. So, rather than make a conscious decision about wall colour, let your handmade pieces become the focal point and choose a neutral background to set them against.

As with so many things in life, the best approach is to keep things simple. Choose soft 'non-colour' hues, such as off-whites, light blues and shades of grey, that will create a colour palette that is as tempting as blobs of gently melting ice cream. These quiet, tranquil hues will have their own moment of glory as a backdrop to more edgy and colourful handmade objects. As the light changes, the tones will brighten, sharpen and soften, depending on the time of day. These are colours that don't tend to go in and out of fashion, so they are comforting and easy to live with and help to create a calm, peaceful atmosphere.

THIS PAGE Delicately painted ceramic pebbles by Devon-based artist Clare Mahoney sit on top of a pair of linen cushions by Berlin textile designer Margarete Häusler. They have been dip dyed in a vat of Yves Klein blue that matches perfectly the hand-woven Indian fringed shawl underneath.

OPPOSITE BELOW A collection of jewellery has found the perfect home in a carved wooden block from Africa. Such pieces were often used on market stalls to hold money, like a till drawer. The beads are wrapped in remnants of silk, a good example of recycling. The silver rings are by French and English silversmiths.

You will find that your paintings, pictures, ceramics and textiles will provide flashes of colour and, inevitably, the dominant colours will slowly manifest themselves in unexpected and unplanned ways. Soon you will realize that a colour scheme is gradually developing and the objects you surround youself with are in tonal harmony, even if they weren't consciously chosen for that reason.

Take a good look at the bare bones of your house, too. If you've got beautiful wooden floors (or wooden floors that have the potential to be beautiful) and walls that are coated in layer upon layer of paint, then your luck is in and your decorating solutions are just waiting for you to get your paint scraper out and find them. For a long time, our favourite approach to decoration has been what we call 'domestic archaeology': scraping paint off doors, walls and furniture and taking a peep at what lies hidden beneath, the relics of previous generations of decorators. If it looks promising, keep going – this is a great way of working with

ABOVE A folded green Welsh waffle blanket from Damson and Slate is slung casually over these banisters, on hand for chilly nights. Its gently undulating tones of green, along with the extra vibrant flash of green stitched along the edge, mirror the colours of the flaky painted green wood panels beyond. Together, they brighten up the stairway without trying too hard.

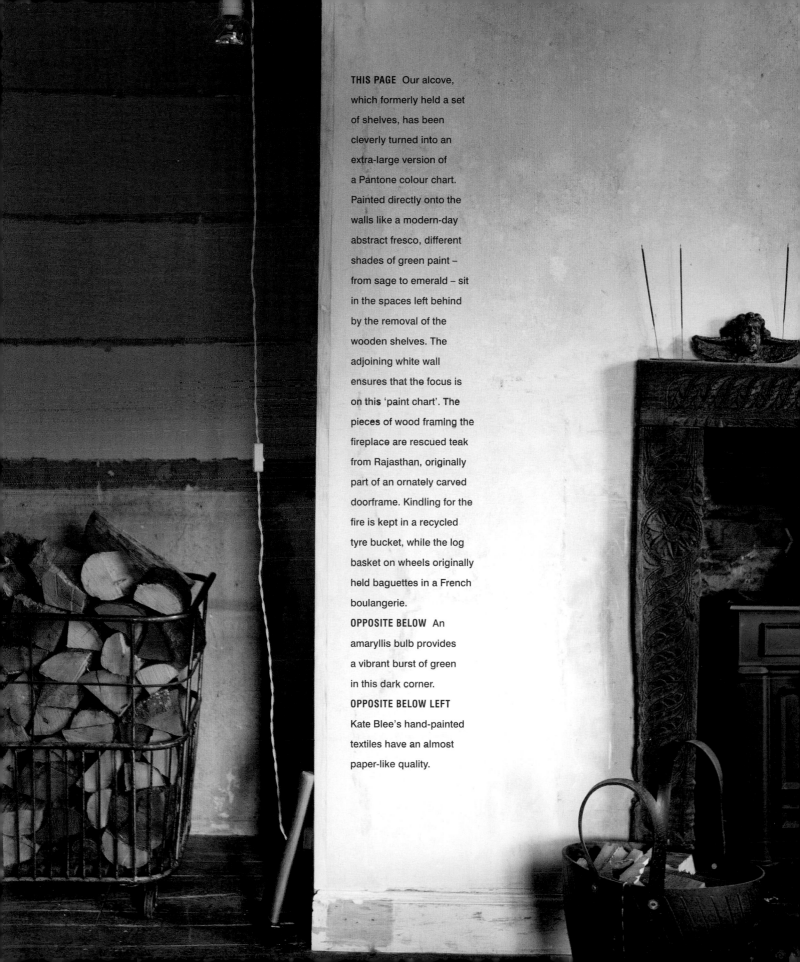

THIS PAGE Our alcove, which formerly held a set of shelves, has been cleverly turned into an extra-large version of a Pantone colour chart. Painted directly onto the walls like a modern-day abstract fresco, different shades of green paint – from sage to emerald – sit in the spaces left behind by the removal of the wooden shelves. The adjoining white wall ensures that the focus is on this 'paint chart'. The pieces of wood framing the fireplace are rescued teak from Rajasthan, originally part of an ornately carved doorframe. Kindling for the fire is kept in a recycled tyre bucket, while the log basket on wheels originally held baguettes in a French boulangerie.

OPPOSITE BELOW An amaryllis bulb provides a vibrant burst of green in this dark corner.

OPPOSITE BELOW LEFT Kate Blee's hand-painted textiles have an almost paper-like quality.

LEFT Old mirrors dulled with age and with speckled silvering have been reworked by the Baileys workshop and given a new lease of life on a variety of different industrial legs.
RIGHT This room has been painted in blocks of various shades of yellow, ranging from a muted straw tone to a rectangle of vibrant sunflower yellow. The blocks create an abstract effect, almost like a Mark Rothko painting.

colour rather than imposing it (and is so much more satisfying than weekends spent deliberating over a paint chart).

Peeling off layers of paint and wallpaper can reveal interesting flashes of colour and texture that tell the story of your home's many past lives. Not all of the exposed decorative schemes will appeal, but don't be afraid of gaudily bright remnants from the 1960s or 70s – you never know what they could spark off, or what in your collection of art and craft they might work with. A few words of warning, though – if peeling and scraping turns out to be your thing, don't get too carried away. Scrape down the walls, by all means, but keep the woodwork smooth or vice versa – it's contrasting textures and finishes that keep a room interesting and prevent it from being overwhelmed by too many similar textures.

OPPOSITE A favourite pair of brown leather shoes wait patiently on the stairs beside a bright macramé bag woven by a Fairtrade women's cooperative. The vibrancy of the bag enhances the drab speckled yellow of the scuffed painted boards – a perfect example of the wonderful effects that wear and tear can have, if you're prepared to live with them! The stair runner has been removed, leaving a pleasing striped effect up the staircase.
RIGHT Soft skeins of dyed Drenthe Heath sheep wool hang down in colourful lengths, creating their own decorative display while they wait to be used.

BELOW LEFT A group of almost fluorescent yarns contrasts with the gentle greens of the painting above. The softer pink reel makes a good introduction to the group and provides the eye with a necessary counterbalance to the brighter tones.

BELOW CENTRE Delicate handmade paper jewellery by Ana Hagopian hangs from utilitarian metal hooks as well as a vintage cotton reel. The necklaces make for a colourful and sculptural display resting against the white painted wooden boards. The purple necklace is the odd one out that brings the others into sharper focus.

BELOW RIGHT An odd assortment of objects, including a white plaster hand and an abstract expressionist painted stone, are brought together by their similar colours. The red paint behind them ensures their whiteness stands out from the crowd.

OPPOSITE An amazingly vibrant pile of fabrics by Dutch textile artist Claudy Jongstra demonstrates the astonishing hues that can be achieved using natural dyes. The inclusion of the purple and blue pieces towards the top of the pile has the effect of sharpening our appreciation of the brighter cadmium reds and scarlets. The different textures in the pile also enhance the tonal values of the colours.

Nature is another way to introduce colour into your home. Natural materials such as wood and stone only improve with the passage of time, as their colours mellow with age or exposure to the elements. Wood brings a feeling of solidity and timelessness, and it is a great anchor to softly painted walls. Wooden floors feel pleasant underfoot and their grain, colour and texture will warm up white-washed walls. Wooden panelling or recycled wooden boards will add another dimension to your walls. Pieces of sun-bleached driftwood are reminders of wood in its natural form and add alternative tones and character to a natural palette. The same is true of holiday collections of beach pebbles.

Plants and 'unarranged' fresh flowers are another way to bring in colour: the zesty brights of midsummer flowers are perfect for the dazzling light and long days, while Mother Nature knows how to tone it down in winter, with bluey-green evergreens and pops of vibrantly coloured berries here and there.

While gentle colour tones provide the perfect backdrop, there is also room for the occasional, well-considered bright splash of paint. Masking off a small area of wall just behind a display and painting it in a more flamboyant colour can be a way of showcasing and uniting a group of disparate, unconnected objects. Just make sure it's always done in moderation.

TEXTURE

TEXTURE COULD BE CONSIDERED THE BADGE OF HONOUR OF THE HANDMADE HOME: IT SPEAKS OF THE HAND OF THE MAKER. EQUALLY, TEXTURE GIVES EVIDENCE OF AGE AND USE. WHILE SLEEK, SHINY MANUFACTURED SURFACES HAVE THEIR PLACE, THEY CRY OUT TO BE OFFSET BY MORE ACTIVE, UNEVEN TEXTURES. CONTRASTING TEXTURES WILL BRING VITALITY AND INTEREST TO AN INTERIOR; THEY'LL MAKE YOU STOP AND LOOK (AND, MORE THAN LIKELY, REACH OUT AND TOUCH TOO).

ABOVE LEFT This section
of wall has been left bare,
showing off its rough-
and-ready stone and lime-
based pointing. In front,
a daybed has been neatly
made up with a beautiful
blue blanket and topped
with a cushion made from
a striped Hungarian linen
grain sack.
ABOVE RIGHT A hank of
natural undyed wool from
Claudy Jongstra's wild and
woolly sheep has an
appealingly tactile quality
that makes you want to
reach out and stroke it.

Texture plays an important role in the handmade home. Without a variety of textures, an interior will feel strangely one-dimensional and uninspiring. Texture brings richness, depth and warmth to a home and renders it appealing to the senses. However, it's important to have a considered balance of textures – both the rough and the smooth, the glossy and the crumpled. Too much of one texture without any counterpoint will feel soulless and overwhelming (or in some cases, underwhelming might be a better word) – think of a bland hotel room full of over-upholstered shiny cushions and bedcovers or an airport lounge full of stark hard edges with nothing to relieve or soften them.

Achieving the perfect balance of textures is not an exact science – you need to look, touch and experiment in order to find out what goes where and with what. Mixing up textures encourages you to appreciate the innate properties of different materials. In general, the key is to think opposites – dress a sofa upholstered in coarse undyed linen with a couple of plump, soft cushions, or cover a hard wooden floor with a thick, long-pile rug so you can wriggle your toes in its generous depths.

Fabric will introduce comfort and warmth into your home. For a welcoming, relaxed vibe, place casual piles of folded blankets on the end of a bed or over the back of a chair or sofa.

THIS PAGE This cosy fireplace with a space to sit and soak up the warmth, is a fine example of contrasting textures. The plaster surrounding the fireplace has been coloured by mixing pigment into the clay; it has then been trowelled on to create extra texture. The polished slate hearth provides a sleek contrast to the rough walls, while a blanket made of shaggy Drenthe Heath wool and a felted cushion soften the blunt edges.

THIS PAGE In this well-organized kitchen, the utensils have been separated by material: wood and metal. The shiny stainless steel shelf contrasts with the pitted finish of the frosted glass, which allows dappled light to filter through.

ABOVE LEFT Layers of paint and a bright scorch mark are reminiscent of mossy tree bark.

ABOVE RIGHT A collection of turned wooden plates and bowls sit among piles of Indian marble and pewter on an old wooden dresser.

LEFT The wooden bones of this timber-framed long barn have a beautiful tactile natural texture, which adds warmth to the room.

RIGHT The tones of wood in both its natural state and scruffy painted boards warm the cold slate floor.

It feels friendly and welcoming, assuring any visitor that they will feel toasty and warm, whatever the weather. In the handmade home, natural fabrics are always the best fit – undyed or naturally dyed wool, cotton, linen and jute are much more appealing than man-made artificial textiles.

Texture extends well beyond fabric, however. If you are lucky enough to have a brick or stone wall in your home, resist the temptation to 'finish' it with a smooth layer of plaster. Left uncovered, unfinished stone is a perfect counterpoint to plastered walls, revealing the bare bones and highlighting the underlying structure of your home. On the subject of plaster, consider alternatives to the norm. Lime plaster has a tactile pale and chalky finish, whereas clay plaster gives a pleasantly pitted texture,

reminiscent of orange peel or a handmade stoneware jug, which makes you want to touch it – not something that can often be said about a plastered wall! Both types of plaster should be left unpainted, in order to showcase their unique finishes.

Concrete is another material worthy of consideration. The name conjures up images of dull paving slabs or oppressive 1960's tower blocks, but concrete has so much more going for it than its image would suggest. The gritty rawness of concrete has a handcrafted quality and provides a perfect contrast to many other textures, especially fabrics, glass and handmade ceramics.

Find a skilled concrete craftsman, and you'll be amazed by the results. Consider using concrete to build shelves or storage units, or use it in place of wooden panels or wallpaper on your

OPPOSITE ABOVE A raw looking concrete shelf retains an imprint of the knotty texture from the wood used in the moulding process. It is home to various vessels of differing texture, including a recycled glass carafe, a stoneware bottle and a chunky old French chopping board that leans against the smooth lime-plastered wall. A couple of Ethiopian wooden bowls, probably once used for milking, look more like over-sized coffee cups in this domestic setting. A bowl by a Majorcan potter holds liquorice sticks.

ABOVE A hand-stitched book by artist Kate Blee has an amazing sculptural quality, especially when seen beside its flatter cousins. The edges have been dipped in ink, giving it the feel of a favourite novel left out in the rain.

walls. Concrete structures are created using wooden shuttering to mould the poured concrete and keep it in place while it is drying. The exciting part comes when the shuttering is removed – it's rather like unwrapping a present, as you can never quite predict what you're going to find! As the concrete sets, the knots and grain of the wood become subtly imprinted on to the surface, along with other unexpected marks and tiny air pockets. The excitement doesn't stop there, either – as concrete dries and cures, it lightens in colour. Poured concrete floors always look impressive, and they will develop a pleasing patina of age. The worst that can happen is that you run out of concrete before you've finished pouring the floor, so make sure you hire someone who gets all the calculations right!

Unlike concrete, wood is imbued with a sense of tradition – people have been crafting wooden furniture for many centuries. Wood has warmth, honesty and a feeling of solidity and permanence. It ages beautifully and is surprisingly versatile – with a little imagination and some basic carpentry skills, wooden pieces can easily be recycled. Next time you find yourself rummaging through a salvage yard, don't worry too much about the function or condition of a piece. Instead, think like a craftsman who chooses his material with care and attention and see the items as raw materials that can be given a new lease of life.

When you're a keen collector of handmade objects, it's important to have plenty of surfaces on which to display your treasures. Concrete, stone and wooden shelves make ideal backdrops, as they have a natural affiliation with the innate qualities of handmade pieces, making them both look and feel perfectly at home. However, don't turn your back on man-made materials, such as stainless steel, mirrors or glass. Such sleek and reflective surfaces also have their place and will prove a foil to handmade textures, such as loosely woven baskets, chunky unglazed pots or delicate, porous porcelain.

ABOVE LEFT Scraps of brightly coloured wool spun from the fleeces of Claudy Jongstra's sheep have been twisted to form vibrant textural necklaces. They have the appearance of intriguing and sculptural artworks hung on the knobs of a cupboard door, proving that art can be anything you choose it to be. Their clashing colours and knobbly textures are enhanced by the smoothly painted white wooden boards.

ABOVE CENTRE A large wooden bowl holds a collection of brightly coloured, heavily textured string that comes all the way from Nepal. The array of vibrant colours really stands out from the worn wood.

ABOVE RIGHT AND OPPOSITE A thin cushion made using pieces of reworked coarse jute sacking has been sewn together using oversized stitches of bright rainbow coloured wool. The cushion was made during a children's craft workshop in The Art Shop, a small gallery and art supply shop located in the south Wales market town of Abergavenny. The clumsy stitches in vibrant shades are surprisingly beautiful, and give the cushion a primitive, almost tribal feel. The contrastingly traditional design of the chair on which the cushion now sits highlights the simplicity of the handmade creation.

TEXTILES

THE WORLD OF TEXTILES IS IMBUED WITH GREAT HERITAGE, TRADITION AND

CRAFTSMANSHIP – SPINNING, WEAVING, DYEING AND EMBROIDERY ARE JUST A FEW

OF THE SKILLS THAT HAVE BEEN HANDED DOWN THROUGH THE GENERATIONS. TODAY,

MUCH OF THIS EXPERTISE IS KEPT ALIVE BY TEXTILE ARTISTS, AND WHAT WERE ONCE

CONSIDERED TO BE HUMBLE CRAFTS NOW RESULT IN HIGHLY COLLECTABLE WORKS

OF ART. RECONSIDER HOW YOU USE TEXTILES IN YOUR HOME AND TRY HANGING RUGS,

QUILTS OR OTHER WOVEN PIECES ON THE WALL AS ARTWORKS IN THEIR OWN RIGHT.

Whether you choose to display them as works of art or put them to work in a more traditional role, textiles are a great way to bring colour and texture to your home. They soften the architectural edges of a room and give it warmth and personality without trying too hard.

Ever-so-slightly untidy piles of blankets and throws casually stacked on the end of a bed or thrown over the back of an armchair are often small works of art in themselves, with their casually overlapping edges and tangled fringes creating tactile layers of colour and texture. In the handmade home, it is best to keep textiles as close to their natural state as possible. Undyed fabrics or those hand-dyed with natural dyes in vibrant hues, exposed stitching and unfinished edges are just the kind of details expected in a home that's a hymn to craftsmanship and artisan makers.

Graceful yet understated, vintage linen in neutral hues of putty and oatmeal has endless uses. More and more Eastern European linen seems to be finding

OPPOSITE LEFT The sheer curtain in this minimally furnished Japanese living space softens the light that filters in through the large window. The angular armchair and its matching stool have been upholstered in a more sturdy linen fabric.

OPPOSITE RIGHT Piles of softly fringed blankets are kept close at hand to provide extra winter warmth – often necessary in the long Scandinavian winters, where this scene is set. The undyed natural hues of the blankets and the tangled fringing contrast with the sensible solidity of the deep inky blue modular sofa. An undyed piece of Hungarian linen sacking has been made into a simple cushion cover.

OPPOSITE BELOW Remnants of freshly laundered French vintage linen are held in place with a trio of heart-shaped stones collected from Norfolk beaches.

THIS PAGE A pile of linen dyed in various shades of blue sit patiently on a heavily textured wooden bench in this tranquil bedroom. A string of heavy purple glass tribal beads lie on top of the pile, anchoring it in place and adding another, smoother surface to the arrangement.

THIS PAGE Panels of undyed natural cotton canvas have been used to section off a small sleeping area in this open-plan barn conversion. The canvas sheets are attached to a wooden framework using loops of thick string threaded through metal eyelets. It gives a seductive feeling of camping, with all the positive connotations of outdoor living that this brings but none of the bad weather!

OPPOSITE ABOVE LEFT A utilitarian-looking small metal peg has been used to hold a pair of tobacco coloured curtains closed.

RIGHT A simple pair of patchwork curtains has been made by stitching together natural linen tea towels with cheerful pieces of purple and white checked gingham.

BELOW Rectangular pieces of sheer fabrics in various sizes have been stitched together to create this sheer curtain, which allows daylight to filter through the long window. The graphic pattern built up by the layers of rectangles is reminiscent of an abstract painting by Paul Klee.

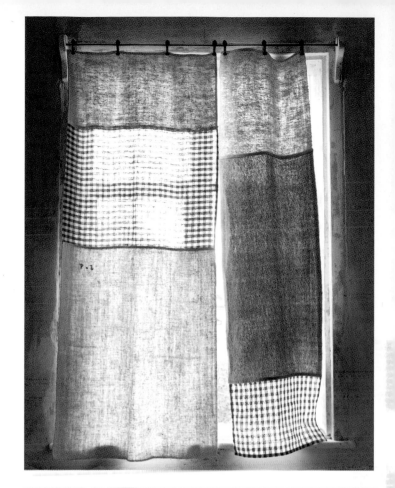

its way to vintage markets and fairs. It tends to be more substantial and robust than its finer French cousin, yet its quiet colouring and simplicity makes it the perfect partner to more luxurious or patterned fabrics. Hungarian grain sacks, cart covers or even the humble tea towel, often found with the traditional red or blue stripe, can be refashioned into cushions of all shapes and sizes. If you come across some hardworking hemp, snap it up to cover a chair in need of reupholstering – look for linens with a close weave, as these work best. Don't worry if vintage linen has small holes or marks; it adds to the fabric's charm and character. Vintage or new but traditional-looking linens with folksy embroidery are something to keep an eye out for too. French linen is the ultimate in elegantly understated bedding. It looks even better as it ages, with soft crumpling and creasing, and has a pleasing coolness that's perfect for warmer evenings. Vintage pieces often come with intricately embroidered monograms, which give a sense of a piece's history.

Canvas is another hard-wearing and utilitarian fabric. It can be used as a space divider – either punch it with eyelets and thread it onto cord, or make it into informal curtains with a tab-top heading. Artists' canvas, available by the metre from good art shops, is ideal for an unfussy tablecloth that can be thrown over a table either

indoors or out. And if you feel creative, so much the better – it's made to be painted on. Linen and canvas both take dye well, and there are many short courses on offer that teach the techniques of natural dyeing. The results are often surprisingly vibrant. Especially pleasing are inky indigo blues, which provide a rich foil to the neutral hues of linen and canvas. Flashes of bright yellow and orange can also be achieved through the use of natural dyes and will really perk up a room.

Floaty sheer fabrics hung at a window will play with the light as it changes through the day. Make a curtain by patching scraps of sheer fabric together to create a graphic abstract pattern that Klee or Mondrian would be proud of. It's a quick and easy way of introducing a handmade element. Don't be afraid of showing your workmanship either – the stitching is the signature of the maker, which is what makes an item unique. The number of patches you use will be dictated not only by the size of your window but also the amount of patience you have when it comes to handstitching!

Textiles are extremely versatile and crying out to be turned into works of art – dyeing, felting, weaving, plaiting and knotting are just a few of the techniques used by textile artists, who create sculptural 3-D pieces from the very simplest of starting points. Intricately woven antique rugs are too good to walk on, and make beautiful wall-hangings. However, when considering textiles as art don't just go for the obvious – vintage clothes, especially old costumes or uniforms, can make just as much of a statement when hung on the wall.

ABOVE An example of the beautiful and vibrant textiles created by artist Kate Blee (see pages 88–95). She paints dye directly onto the fabric, which she then finishes with a fixative to keep the dyes under control. This unusual technique ensures that her work is always spontaneous, experimental and unique. Kate uses a broad colour palette and is not afraid to experiment with more unusual colour combinations.

OPPOSITE In Kate's bright studio, a dark-hued piece of linen that's been newly painted a rich purpley-blue shade has been pegged out to dry on an indoor washing line, hanging alongside some of its more colourful cousins.

OPPOSITE A heap of dyed textiles by Claudy Jongstra brightens up a dark shelf. Claudy's work tends to be on a grand scale – these are experimental practice pieces of her handmade felt. This selection of vibrant yellow samples have the percentages of the natural dyes used to colour them scribbled on the back. A piece of orange felt just peeking out at the bottom of the pile heightens the impact of the bright colours.

THIS PAGE Here a definite theme has been decided on. A yellow jacket, originally part of the wardrobe of a theatre company, has been given pride of place in this display – it feels as if the coat has plenty of tales to tell. The cleanly painted sunny yellow wall is in contrast with the frayed edges and exposed stitches of the jacket. A string of yellow African beads add to the vibrancy of the ensemble.

MADE
BY HAND

INTRODUCING ELEMENTS OF THE HANDMADE INTO YOUR HOME WILL MAKE SURE YOU STAND OUT FROM THE CROWD. WHEN SOMETHING IS MADE BY HAND IT IS TOTALLY UNIQUE – NO MATTER HOW HARD THE MAKER MIGHT TRY TO MAKE A REPLICA, THE WAY HE OR SHE HOLDS THE BRUSH, MOULDS THE CLAY OR GRIPS THE PENCIL WILL ALTER SLIGHTLY FROM PIECE TO PIECE. THIS 'PERFECT IMPERFECTION' IS WHAT MAKES THE HANDMADE INCREASINGLY SOUGHT-AFTER.

PREVIOUS A trio of delightful handmade apples by artist Eiko Yoshida, who originally trained as a jewellery designer. In making these apples Eiko uses recycled paper, magazines, envelopes (complete with stamps) and corrugated card, all combined with gnarly twigs of apple wood.
LEFT Three Ethiopian bowls carved from single blocks of wood by tribal craftsmen have the cartoon-like appearance of extra-large tea and coffee cups.
BELOW Edla Griffiths's sculptural earthenware jugs are hand-built using the slab and coil method then decorated with scratched and painted surface designs. The three slipware jugs on the left are by Jane Bowen.

There was a time, not that long ago, when a love of craft was not something you would necessarily want to shout from the rooftops. Craft, and the wonkily handmade, was marginalized and overlooked in favour of new, uniform and perfectly shiny mass-produced goods. Happily, that is no longer the case and it is refreshing to see that craft is enjoying a renaissance of popularity, what with ceramicist Grayson Perry winning the Turner prize in 2003 and the rise of websites such as Etsy, which is like having an international craft fair at your fingertips (and a really good one at that). Bookshops and newsagents are full of books and magazines on all types of arts and crafts. Origin – an annual contemporary craft fair held in Spitalfields market as part of the London Design Festival – has taken 'Made Not Manufactured' as its motto and gets busier and busier year by year. A handmade object is made with discernable care and attention: the

OPPOSITE This pair of unusual bottle vases were bought at a flea market by Leslie Oschmann and are similar to ones she remembers making as a child. The unusual flower heads that poke out from the top are fashioned from any scraps of canvas left over from Leslie's main work, with stamens made from spent brushes.

maker takes creative pleasure in the design and making process and the buyer values their skill and the beauty and individuality of the finished piece. Handcrafted items cannot be produced in large quantities and there is much to be said for quality over quantity. Increasingly, we are embracing individuality, rejecting assembly-line goods and moving away from chain stores, which can only be a good thing.

Handmade means different things to different people. There are those artefacts that sit on a shelf or hang on a wall, there to be admired for their beauty and the skill of the artist or the maker. But as well as these undeniable delights, there are many other ways in which the handmade can enter into your everyday life, from teacups to cushions to chairs. Drinking tea from a handmade mug brings you into direct contact with the object,

adding an enjoyable element to an everyday routine and allowing a daily appreciation of its unique nature. Don't leave crafting to other people either – it's good to learn a new skill, such as pottery or weaving, and it is really satisfying to create something that enhances your surroundings.

Look out for old crafts too, and cherish objects that were made by hand quite simply because that was the only method available at the time, such as roughly hewn wooden bowls, or drinking vessels carved from a single piece of wood. These items were made to last, so keep on using them however you can, even if it's not in the way that was originally intended. These things deserve to be admired just because they have survived, so stand them on a shelf alongside your favourite delicate handmade ceramics – the contrast will add an extra dimension to both.

OPPOSITE LEFT A wobbly handcarved Ethiopian wooden bowl holds a collection of slightly battered copper and brass watering-can roses. The copper ones have developed a verdigris patina over time and use. These sculptural-looking roses have been made by hand as far back as the 18th century.

OPPOSITE RIGHT A hand-thrown teapot and mug by potter John Leach sit on a three-legged Welsh stool. John Leach's pots are left unglazed on the exterior, allowing the flames of the kiln to create a 'toasted' texture and finish.

ABOVE LEFT Over time, this large brass cooking bowl has been repaired with neat patches. With age, these honest repairs have become an integral part of the object's beauty.

ABOVE RIGHT Strainers made from woven recycled paper have a timeless quality and look as if they could be as old as the roughly hewn wooden bowls from Ethiopia in which they sit.

RIGHT A quirky group of handmade bits and pieces. At the back of the line is a handmade apple by Eiko Yoshida, followed by a ball of twisted paper string. An over-sized hammered iron nail is next, alongside a few bleached twigs. At the front is a string of chunky wooden beads.

BELOW When former visual director of Anthroplogie, Leslie Oschmann moved from America to Amsterdam, she started to scour the flea markets of Europe and built up a collection of old oil paintings of forgotten portraits and landscapes, as well as pieces of furniture that had seen better days. Leslie thoughtfully reworks all her finds, covering old chairs, tables, cupboards – any furniture of any scale that she can find, in fact – in stitched patchwork pieces of the paintings.

BELOW LEFT Here a crackled and battered painting of a sadly long-forgotten lady takes on a new lease of life, soon to be cherished once again. Until that time comes, the bag is pegged in place with a sturdy easel clip.

BELOW CENTRE Leslie is careful to use all the odds and ends of the paintings. Here, some smaller pieces have been stitched together to create a beautiful but functional pencil case.

BELOW RIGHT The painted tubular steel of this functional looking chair is complimented by fragments of a blue oil painting, which have been collaged onto its curved wooden seat and back.

OPPOSITE RIGHT Wooden shoe lasts sit on a shelf holding smouldering incense sticks.

Honest mending and repairs are also something to be admired, as are scratches, dents and other signs of wear and tear – all part of the patina of age. Beauty can be found in the most unexpected places – even pieces of hand-forged hardware such as nails and hinges and old wooden tools have a certain charm of their own.

Recycling is another way to introduce the handmade into your life, although this sort of recycling is a long way from putting piles of newspaper on the doorstep once a week. Think creative – don't discard an item just because it has seen better days but consider what you (or someone else) could do with it. Adding a set of casters to some crates to create a coffee table or adding a wooden top to an old metal washtub to transform it into a table will completely change the function of an object. Old brioche tins or kilner jars can become lampshades and pieces of scaffolding can be used to make bed frames. Portraits of long-forgotten figures painted on canvas can be transformed into bags and seat covers. Tools and functional furniture from the days when things were made by hand by skilled craftsman deserve a long and productive retirement: bobbins can become string or scissor holders, for example, while pieces of print block can be recycled as blind pulls or drawer handles – all it takes is an appreciation of their practical beauty and the vision to see them in a new light.

LEFT A group of industrial objects from long-outdated factories and production processes are grouped together on a pair of shoe trolleys that have been given a new life with the addition of new wooden shelves. The top two shelves are home to a variety of solid-looking wooden hat blocks. Below them are wooden bobbins rescued from defunct cotton mills, alongside a spiky board designed to hold smaller cotton reels.

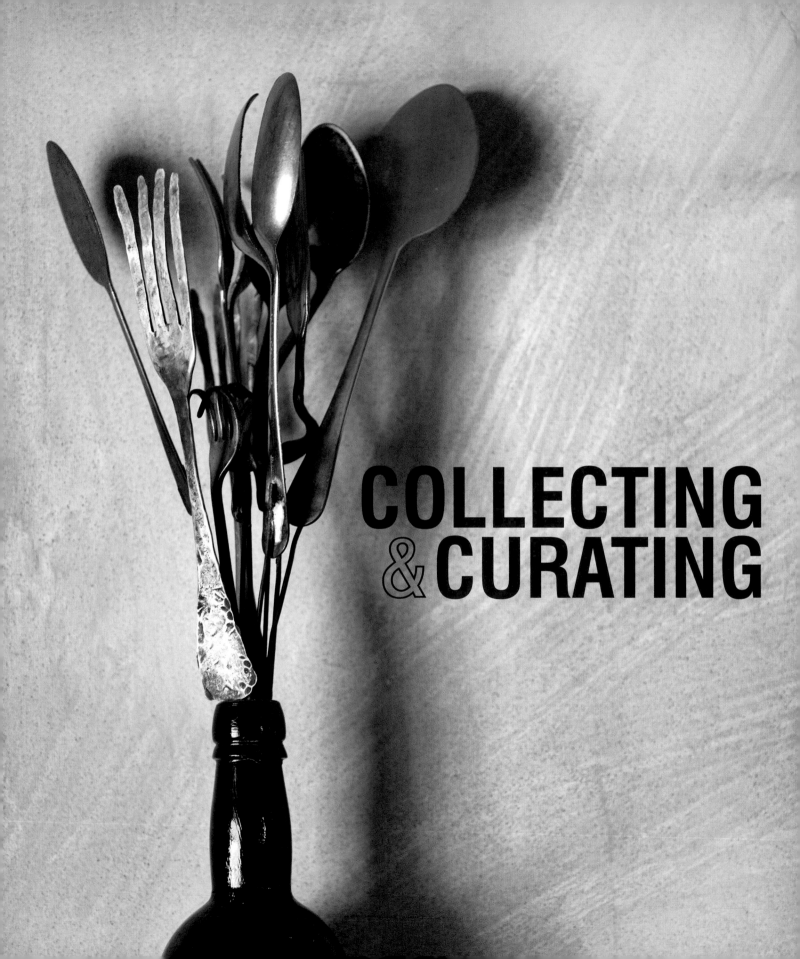

COLLECTING
& CURATING

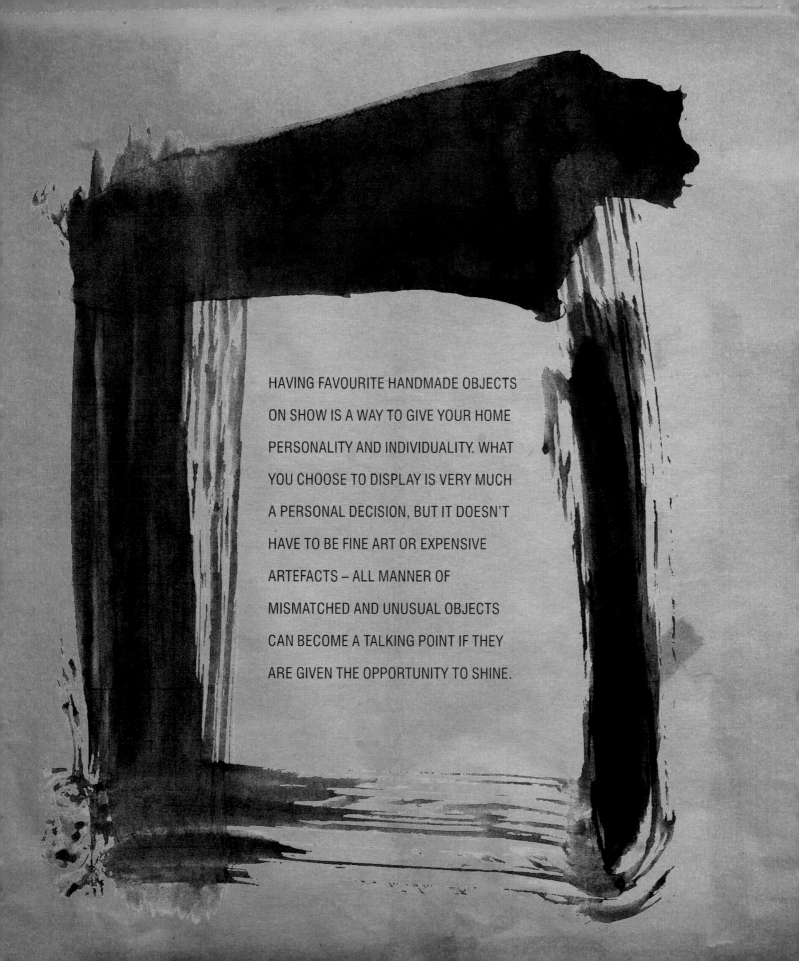

HAVING FAVOURITE HANDMADE OBJECTS
ON SHOW IS A WAY TO GIVE YOUR HOME
PERSONALITY AND INDIVIDUALITY. WHAT
YOU CHOOSE TO DISPLAY IS VERY MUCH
A PERSONAL DECISION, BUT IT DOESN'T
HAVE TO BE FINE ART OR EXPENSIVE
ARTEFACTS – ALL MANNER OF
MISMATCHED AND UNUSUAL OBJECTS
CAN BECOME A TALKING POINT IF THEY
ARE GIVEN THE OPPORTUNITY TO SHINE.

LEFT A grouping of vintage
French coal shovels are held
in place on a well-ordered
utilitarian clip rack.
BELOW LEFT A collection of
children's boots, shoes and
clogs have found the perfect
resting spot in the pigeonholes
of this old French post cabinet,
which has been freshened up
with a lick of white paint.
RIGHT A line of heart-shaped
pebbles collected from Norfolk
beaches makes a quirky display
on a bleached wooden table.

There are many different reasons why we collect things, but if you
take time to consider the way in which you display your collections,
your treasures will take on a whole new life. Something magical starts
to happen when you think about how to group your favourite things:
they create focal points; areas of interest in your home that irresistibly
draw the eye. Thematic groupings of paintings, prints or 3-D objects
will create a more interesting dialogue than a haphazard arrangement
and allow seemingly unconnected objects to sit happily together. Start
by putting together those objects that share similar materials, colours
or subjects and then consider where and how to display them.

For affordable art, look out for end-of-year art shows at colleges
and open studios and art fairs, where you are likely to pick up a
bargain and perhaps meet the artist too. Hang prints and paintings in
clusters, rather than in a long line, art-gallery style (this is also a useful
technique if you have limited wall space). Keep the gaps between the
frames approximately the same size, and the grouping will look
planned rather than higgledy-piggledy, and will also allow
mismatched frames to coexist harmoniously.

For a more relaxed approach to art display, prop pictures up
against the wall on a chest of drawers or desk – perhaps overlap
the frames slightly, inviting closer inspection on the part of the viewer.

THIS PAGE A clean white shed has been turned into a miniature shoe museum! An old French workbench provides the ideal place for a row of traditional clogs, still made by hand In Yorkshire to this very day. Hung on the wooden planks behind are wooden sock and stocking forms, which would once have graced the laundry room of a grand country house. Here, they are held in place by a row of metal pegs which also incorporates vintage cotton reels that have been given a new job to do.

OPPOSITE A set of stainless-steel shelves provides polished contrast to the lime-plastered walls on which they hang. They hold a collection of wooden objects, including polished vessels and small jewellery boxes by seasoned woodturner Ray Key, who uses a variety of different woods in his work. The wooden apples are vintage finds.

ABOVE LEFT Recycled glass beads hold two necklaces made from Nepalese paper by Argentinean designer Ana Hagopian. The one on the right resemble a bunch of flowers hung up to dry.

ABOVE RIGHT A collection of Dylan Bowen plates, their monochrome abstract swirls the perfect partner to a set of vintage cricket scoring numbers.

RIGHT Paper plates have been daubed with abstract expressionist drips and swirls then mounted and simply framed.

FAR RIGHT A wooden shelf holds two sycamore plates by Ray Key as well as several John Leach plates and mugs. The giant aluminium fork was once part of an advertisement for a café or restaurant.

Larger pieces will be happy on the floor, and leaning work on shelves is also a good way to make sure all your art gets an airing as it saves the hassle of rehanging – all that's required is a reshuffle every so often, to keep displays fresh and inspiring. You can also place complementary pieces on the shelf for a more 3-D display.

A collection doesn't necessarily have to be made up of specific art objects, such as paintings, ceramics or sculptures. Found objects from the natural world such as shells, pebbles or driftwood can also form the foundation for an interesting display. Intriguingly patterned or shaped pebbles or shells look good on a bare wooden floor or artfully arranged on a flight of stairs. You can also elevate the status of natural objects by placing them in front of empty frames that have lost their original pictures or by covering them with glass domes or cloches, thus suggesting they are precious works of art and encouraging viewers to see them in a different light.

Beautifully made industrial objects from the past make for great displays and deserve to be appreciated for their superior craftsmanship. Showcase these vintage gems in a way that reflects their utilitarian past – a clip rack could hold a row of vintage garden tools, while a chunky wooden workbench is

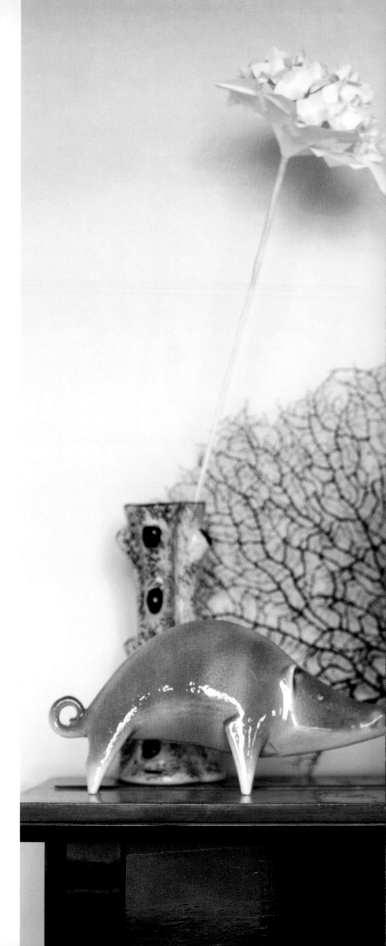

OPPOSITE ABOVE A collection of jewellery made up of hammered silver and carved wooden bangles, is displayed on an unusual array of green painted cones, which would once have held single floral stems in a florist's shop.

LEFT Ceramic animals and a couple of woollen birds form a happy crowd on top of a piano, patiently waiting for someone to strike up a tune. A lacy piece of coral and a delicate origami paper flower stuck in an unusual tree trunk-like vase add to the naturalistic theme of this group.

ABOVE A collection of folky pottery, including a beautiful internally glazed colander with stubby feet and an earthenware bread crock, make up a tranquil still life on a limed oak tabletop. The sketches by Fred Ingrams are casually propped against the wall, in keeping with the informality of the drawings and in contrast to the finished paintings, which are hung more formally on the wall above.

a great surface for display. If you're lucky enough to find an old postal cabinet with dozens of pigeonholes, put it into service as a versatile display case. Search art shops and hardware stores for bulldog clips and other similar accessories. As well as working in tandem with industrial objects, they provide contrast when used to hold delicate objects or simple sketches. Your collection will fire the imagination of the viewer in the same way as a well-curated museum display can, but without all the labels or leaflets, making it much more intuitive and fun.

Finding flexible ways of displaying your collections allows you to curate your very own domestic art shows easily and often. As your collections grow and take on a life of their own, the editing process will become more and more important. When it comes to display, less really is more, so rotate your treasures to avoid having everything out on show at the same time. Find some sturdy boxes or wooden crates, get plenty of tissue and think of the cupboard under the stairs as your very own museum vault, with its contents all archived and ready for the next show!

ABOVE LEFT One of Leslie Oschmann's old canvases has been turned the wrong way round to face the wall and is now used as a neutral backdrop against which to display some unusual pendants made using old stencils strung from leather cord.
ABOVE CENTRE The dark oak staircase of The Art Shop and Gallery in Abergavenny, provides the perfect setting for a display of handmade porcelain child's shoes, a

dustpan and brush set with long, spindly handles and a lidded milk pan all by Jessica Hopewell. These beautiful domestic creations stand out in stark contrast to the dark wood.
ABOVE RIGHT A huge collection of delicate ceramic spoons by Helen Felcey are lined up in a dark wooden box in The Art Shop. Some have beautifully curved edges while others sport a striking light blue glaze.

RIGHT A canvas of black hens in the snow by Kumar Saraff has been painted with a broad brush to give a textural quality to the surface of the paint. The shelves of the cabinet beneath hold glazed mugs by Kate Scott and and a ceramic piece in the shape of an old-fashioned grater, which has been decorated with scribbly painted lines by Helen Felcey. At the top of the stairs is a screenprint by William Brown.

THE
HOMES

farmhouse cottage **grain store** barn **townhouse** apartment

OUR LARGE RED SANDSTONE FARMHOUSE IS SET IN THE HEREFORDSHIRE COUNTRYSIDE RIGHT NEXT DOOR TO OUR HOME STORE – PEOPLE OCCASIONALLY WANDER THROUGH FROM THE STORE AND WE HAVE TO WAVE THEM IN THE RIGHT DIRECTION! THIS IS WHERE WE GET THE CHANCE TO EXPERIMENT WITH DISPLAY ON A SMALLER SCALE. WE HAVE LIVED HERE FOR ABOUT SEVEN YEARS AND HAVE SEEN QUITE A FEW CHANGES IN THAT RELATIVELY SHORT SPACE OF TIME. OUR HOME IS WHERE WE EXPERIMENT; IT IS A WORK IN PROGRESS AND NOTHING STAYS THE SAME FOR LONG, SO THERE IS ALWAYS SOMETHING NEW ON OFFER.

BAILEY HOUSE
A 18th-century farmhouse in Herefordshire

PREVIOUS PAGE The framed sketches on the mantelshelf are by Peter Greenaway. The primitive-looking black and white horse painting is by French Canadian artist William Brown. The silvered glass vase is by Alice Cescatti.
ABOVE Pieces of architrave have been pieced together to create this fireplace. A generous Baileys Loft sofa, upholstered in naturally dyed linen, provides a great spot for relaxation.

Along with the barns that make up the store, our house has been sympathetically renovated and restored using recycled and environmentally friendly materials wherever possible. We try not to cover things up and prefer to show what our home has been through over the years. We're big advocates of the philosophy of 'undecoration' – leaving pipework exposed rather than boxed in, and preferring to peel back paint and wallpaper rather than covering the walls in yet another layer of paint. The soft gentle tones of chalky limewash plaster with just revealed speckles of older paint makes the perfect backdrop to our collections of vintage objects and artworks. We do employ the rule of

OPPOSITE BELOW This is the simple kitchen in the rescued tin Tabernacle that we have rebuilt in the grounds of our store. It serves as a café at weekends.

THIS PAGE The floorboards in this room are the original elm boards, but in places they have been patched with pieces of copper and tin. This interior is home to an odd mix of objects, but they are all connected by colour. To add to the effect, the wall has been painted in geometric blocks of varying tones of yellow. The lamp base, which sits on a roughly textured English workbench, was made from an old oil can. Alongside sits a pair of yellow-painted wooden balls. The yellow jacket is hung from a ware board that came from a defunct pottery in Stoke on Trent; it already had its yellow stripes and so slotted into this display with ease.

THIS PAGE Vintage metal American ceiling tiles have been used to cover a wall in the bathroom. They hold just a small selection of Mark's huge collection of vintage garden tools, all of them hand-forged. Look out for tools made by Brades or Ewell, as they are always the best.

contrast here, otherwise it could all get a bit much – some walls are more pristinely painted if we feel it will pull the room together.

We use the house as a home for some of the things we've collected over the years (we've been in business for over 25 years, so we've got a lot of stuff!). Things sometimes move between the farmhouse and the store, so there is a danger it could feel a bit like it's just extra storage space, but we're careful to ensure that anything that is staying in the house for a while is well integrated, rather than standing to one side. It's all about keeping on top of the displays in the house, knowing what's where and making sure we can live with it on a daily basis. There are, however, some things we can't bear to part with, such as Mark's vast collection of vintage garden tools – some of the best ones are currently to be found in our bathroom, held in place in a sturdy looking industrial clip rack.

We have lots of collections of different types of handmade objects in our house – we particularly like stoneware and pretty much anything made of wood, from driftwood or old wooden

ABOVE A modern sink with a shiny Philippe Starck mixer tap sits on an old French table that has clearly spent much of its life outside. An over-sized trowel leans casually against the wall. The mirror frame was once shiny gilt, but has been stripped to reveal its natural beauty.
FAR LEFT Pieces of driftwood used as pegs.
LEFT In this washroom the sink sits atop an old lab worktop. Blackboard panels have been used as cupboard doors.

FAR LEFT A generously deep headboard provides an extra shelf in the bedroom – the perfect resting spot for your bedtime reading.
LEFT A collection of natural wooden objects provides a clue as to the theme of this bedroom.
BELOW Simple shelves provide a display area for a collection of wooden items, from pork pie moulds to an old wooden skittle.

plumber's beads to the most delicate turned wooden bowls. We make lots of things ourselves too – we are constantly searching for pieces of wood or architraving that we can use to make mirror frames, kitchen sink stands, tables or – our most recent favourite – wide, box-like bed headboards. We also have a large collection of vintage textiles, ranging from linen to more ethnic woven pieces, which we use on our beds rather than hiding them away – all part of how we like to live with art every day.

In a house like ours it's important to keep things simple – it could easily get over-full if we didn't keep moving things around. We like to use simple shelving such as folded pieces of paper-thin steel or old wooden boards with very plain wooden brackets, and we arrange displays of items made from similar materials on these shelves. There isn't much colour in our house, other than that which is found in our collected objects, and this provides a calm background for everything else.

THIS PAGE This bedroom is all about our love of wood! The bed and generously proportioned headboard were made in the Baileys workshop using reclaimed wooden boards and steel. Wooden frames that were once coated in gaudy gilt are now given the opportunity to shine, thanks to a quick dip in a vat of caustic soda. A scuffed metal work-in-progress trolley makes a useful bedside table, with extra lighting clipped on to the side. On the other side of the bed, a tubular steel machinist's chair fills the same role.

FOLLOWING PAGE This shed acts as a studio. It's full of all manner of mixed-up objects and the contents change constantly as we come up with new ideas.

LEFT An old Indian table is home to another crazy collection, made up of an old wooden cog that has been given a new lease of life as a mirror. Under the table, a sign saying 'Domestic Bazaar' sums up the scene perfectly.
RIGHT Worn child's chairs sit and hang alongside a table with a recycled wood top on an old sewing machine base.
BELOW RIGHT Metal ceiling tiles make a great magnetic noticeboard.

Q&A (answered by Sally)

What is your favourite travel destination?
Hay-on-Wye on the Welsh Borders and Deia in Mallorca.
We love both places for their stunning setting and artistic and creative vibe and have been visiting them for over 20 years.

Is there anything you would change about your home?
The draughts – Mark has promised to sort them out this year!

What is your favourite book?
The Hare with Amber Eyes by Edmund de Waal – the story of his collection of Japanese netsuke and a journey into family history. We sponsored a talk he gave at the Hay-on-Wye book festival a few years ago, which was fascinating.

Who is your favourite artist/designer?
The Austrian-born studio potter Dame Lucie Rie. I wrote to her once enquiring about buying one of her pots. She wrote a very sweet letter back, but unfortunately she died before I could meet her. We also like the fact that she was renowned for giving any visitors to her London studio tea and cake!

Handmade or mass produced?
Handmade, of course!

THIS PAGE An extra-long wooden bench acts as a low table and holds a beautiful wooden ark. Other wooden toys sit on the window ledge, awaiting the arrival of Priscilla's grandchildren. A bright blue cushion adds a flash of colour to the subdued, relaxed tones of the room.

OPPOSITE ABOVE LEFT The amazing detail of these carved wooden Indian elephants can be clearly seen here.

OPPOSITE BELOW LEFT A vast brick inglenook fire place dominates the room. It would once have served as the heat source for the entire cottage.

OPPOSITE FAR RIGHT A sleek modern woodburning stove is in graphic contrast with the rest of the room, yet the spindly three-legged stools somehow help it fit in.

RURAL COTTAGE

Priscilla Carluccio's rural bolthole in deepest Hampshire

PRISCILLA CARLUCCIO IS ONE OF THE MOST INFLUENTIAL FIGURES IN BRITISH DESIGN. FORMERLY THE WATCHFUL EYE BEHIND HABITAT, HEALS AND THE CONRAN SHOP, SHE IS NOW THE OWNER OF FEW AND FAR ON LONDON'S BROMPTON ROAD. 'THE BOTHY', PRISCILLA'S RURAL BOLTHOLE, IS THE PERFECT EMBODIMENT OF THE HANDMADE HOME ETHOS, WITH ITS PARED-BACK INTERIOR FULL OF OBJECTS AMASSED OVER YEARS OF SEARCHING OUT THE BEST ARTISAN MAKERS.

The Bothy, bought over 20 years ago, was once two cottages dating from the 17th century that have now been brought together as one. What was once the back wall of the cottages is now enclosed by a long corridor that runs across the width of the house, creating a thermos-flask-like double wall that ensures the house is kept cosy or cool, depending on the weather. The kitchen was once an outside shed, but it has since been incorporated into the house and is now home to piles of jelly moulds, fluted cake tins and copper pans, all of which make an impressive display on simple wooden shelves. The unfitted cupboards house stacks of handmade ceramic bowls and global kitchenware such as Moroccan glasses and Greek trays.

The house itself feels handmade, with much of the structure proudly on display and the beams and supports left exposed. The wooden stickback chairs, three-legged stools and spindly tables echo these graphic lines. The walls have been pared back to the original wattle and daub, repaired and patched where necessary by a local plasterer. The house has a beautiful functionality; built using hazel from a nearby wood, clay from a local pond and flint found in neighbouring fields.

ABOVE A group of mismatched classic wooden chairs gather around a round wooden table with sturdy looking legs, designed by Priscilla herself and made by the bespoke furniture company Benchmark.
RIGHT An open shelf in the kitchen is home to neat piles of metal flan and brioche tins, professional-looking copper pans and other precarious towers of cookware.

THIS PAGE A closer inspection of the wooden ark reveals some of the animals peeking out from the boat but also the quality of the craftsmanship – perhaps not that surprising considering that this is the home of someone who has spent her working life tracking down the very finest pieces, handmade by artisan craftsmen across the globe.

LEFT A vintage blue and white patchwork quilt is folded neatly on the edge of a simply clothed bed.
BELOW LEFT Priscilla's collection of woven baskets has been gathered from all over the world and includes an Indian tea picker's basket.
RIGHT Pieces of simple wooden furniture sit comfortably side by side holding piles of well-thumbed books.

The combination of colours, textiles and exposed wood, along with a minimal approach to furnishings, allows the house to suggest a sense of history without being twee, which can be the downfall of many a thatched cottage. There is the occasional splash of colour from a cushion or a jug of country flowers but on the whole the colours are pale and interesting tones of white, which, along with Priscilla's favourite natural fabrics – wool, cotton and linen – create a calming, restful atmosphere that's just the thing when an escape from the busy-ness and noise of London is required.

The artful and considered styling of Priscilla's shop, Few and Far, which provides a collection of internationally sourced clothes along with interesting jewellery, vintage and contemporary furniture, tabletop items and handmade toys to discerning visitors, is also evident in this rural retreat. Priscilla's eye for detail is apparent throughout. There is absolutely nothing extraneous or out of place, but the look is not off-puttingly neat or austere either; rather it is simple and well considered, a gathering of cleanliness and good taste. Objects that appear to be casually thrown together are actually carefully grouped, from a beautiful wooden ark that came from Australia sitting on a long wooden bench that is said to date back to Cromwellian times, to the Wellington boots in various sizes lined up in a row by the door. The house is home to favourite objects that have been amassed over

LEFT AND BELOW A carved Indonesian bath rack rests against the wall in Priscilla's serene bathroom. The fittings are clean and simple, including the old roll-top bath, the outside of which has been painted in a deep greeny-blue shade. The wooden shelf hides the bathroom pipework. An Indonesian carved fish performs an athletic headstand next to a pile of fresh white towels.

many years of hunting out the very best – global artefacts, handmade wooden toys for when the grandchildren pay a visit, and a collection of handwoven baskets in all shapes and sizes hanging from extra-large Shaker-style wooden pegs. The furniture is a combination of large armchairs and comfortable sofas covered in hard-wearing and practical linens alongside a happily mismatched ensemble of traditional wooden country furniture and more contemporary future classics made by Benchmark, a design-led manufacturer of fine bespoke furniture established by Priscilla's brother, Terence Conran.

Nothing in Priscilla's house is too precise or precious but everything feels valued – which is just as it should be.

Q&A

What is your favourite colour combination?
There are so many – blue and white, black and red, collections of brights – it really depends on what it's for.

Which is your favourite room in your home?
The living room and the bedroom and bathroom.

Do you prefer modern or vintage?
I love the mixture of found objects and contemporary – the mixture of materials; of simplicity and complexity.

Which materials do you most like to work with?
Everything, I suppose, depending on its end function!

LEFT A slate from the brook that runs through the back garden rests on a roughly hewn stone sink. A wooden chopping board dries on a pair of wall-mounted lever taps, and a slab of handmade soap hangs just above.
RIGHT Plates by Dylan Bowen in use in the kitchen.
BELOW A stone sink rests on a sturdy wooden table, resulting in an eye-catching combination of rustic sink on refined legs.

GALLERY BAILEY

A home-cum-gallery in a tiny village close to Hay-on-Wye

HAY-ON-WYE IS THE PLACE WE ESCAPE TO – IT MAY SEEM LIKE A BIT OF A LUXURY, BUT LIVING WHERE YOU WORK CAN BE A BIT MUCH SOMETIMES. HOWEVER, OUR BASE IN HAY IS MORE THAN JUST A BOLTHOLE – OUR PLAN IS TO TURN IT INTO A HOME-CUM-GALLERY, GIVING THE HOUSE A CHANCE TO RELIVE ITS ARTISTIC PAST. THE HOUSE WAS ONCE LIVED IN BY ONE OF BRITAIN'S GREATEST DIARISTS, FRANCIS KILVERT. MORE RECENTLY, IT WAS OWNED BY FRIENDS OF OURS: THE ARTIST ELIZABETH ORGAN AND HER PAINTER PARTNER EUGENE FISK WHO BOTH LIVED AND WORKED IN THE HOUSE AND OPENED IT AS A GALLERY FOR THEIR OWN WORK AND THAT OF FRIENDS.

THIS PAGE A traditional looking, no-nonsense Benjamin Franklin stove is framed by an ornate carved surround, which originates from the more exotic climes of Rajasthan, where it was a door frame. There is a pleasing array of colour and texture in this relaxing room from the linen-covered Baileys Loft sofa, and a beautiful handwoven kilim to a rough wooden bowl full of vividly coloured Nepalese string.

THIS PAGE This room is full of handmade objects with all manner of different origins, yet due to their similar natural hues they all sit harmoniously together. There is a mix of ethnic objects, industrial lighting and cushions covered in a very English floral print.

LEFT The vivid green of a Hungarian stoneware jug chimes with a more contemporary piece found at an end-of-year art school show. **RIGHT** The full extent of the green ensemble can be seen here in the former laundry room. An old paint-stained chair has a hint of Jackson Pollock, and works well with the more controlled brush stroke on the plate above. **BELOW RIGHT** A row of painted Hungarian chairs provide a resting spot by the door.

Elizabeth and Eugene also often exhibited the work of budding young artists from Herefordshire, giving them a break in the notoriously difficult art world. They were an inspirational couple for us too, encouraging us in the creative side of our business. When their house came up for sale, we had a 'heart over head' moment, and decided to go for it! Our plan is for this house to become an online gallery, with viewing by appointment and one-off pop-up events. A huge source of inspiration was a trip to Kettle's Yard in Cambridge – a light-filled home where art, much of it from St Ives painters and sculptors (the former owner Jim Ede was curator at the Tate Gallery in the 1920s and '30s), sits contentedly alongside found objects and everyday furniture. Our aim is to fill the house with the handmade combined with the everyday.

The decorative style at the gallery is similar to our farmhouse (see pages 64–71). Once again, we've peeled back layers of paint and paper to see what lies beneath and used chalky limewash plaster. It's been an exciting, almost archaeological process uncovering the marks and lines left behind by old boards, wall-mounted cupboards and shelves. These shaded areas give the walls extra definition and character without the colourful charms of wallpaper or exotic paint charts.

LEFT A group of slightly battered, stripped metal cupboards hang from the lime plastered wall, including one which would once have stood in a dentist's surgery but has been allowed to take the weight off its feet. It now holds a more glamorous display of abstract patterned vessels by one of our favourite ceramicists, Dylan Bowen. **BELOW** An old wooden French wine table placed by a window holds a string of plumber's beads which cast interesting shadows as the light changes throughout the day. An old wooden folding chair sits beside a solid ash stool designed by Alex Hellum. **RIGHT** The shelves are old pew seats that have been cut down and are now held in place with shelf supports designed by Mark and made from very thin stainless steel, which has been folded like a piece of paper. A cheerful gingham tea towel from Fog Linen Work hangs from a spiky wooden hayfork.

The colours here are muted, providing the perfect backdrop to the collection of art and craft that we are in the process of building. The atmosphere feels light and airy, which is especially important in a gallery. The windows are mostly free of dressing – we only use curtains where it's really necessary. Sheer fabrics patched together move in the breeze at the kitchen window, diffusing the light beautifully. The clear light in the house is unobstructed by the furniture, which is made up of leggy stools, slender chairs and simply shaped tables that allow the light to flow over and around them. Lighting is an important consideration too, especially during the darker winter months. We've clipped shiny steel loft lights onto shelves, while the living room boasts a huge 1940's film studio lamp on a wooden tripod. Angular French Jieldé lamps in white are mounted in a sculptural cluster on the ceilings and walls. To provide a flash of colour, our spotlights are hung with brightly coloured, almost fluorescent flex.

THIS PAGE The starting point for this sink stand was an old workbench complete with the handle for a vice still intact – it makes the perfect place for airing tea towels. Doors were attached to the bench with large, smithy-made iron hinges to hide the pipework. The sink on top of the workbench is modern, yet its sturdy, no-nonsense shape ensures it works perfectly with the base.

BELOW A group of old wooden markers, which would have been used in school games such as rounders, stand in an artful row in a kitchen alcove. They bring a splash of colour that relieves the surrounding whiteness.

RIGHT A simple wooden trestle table surrounded by old French bistro chairs, makes for an informal dining spot.

BELOW RIGHT An old American steel ceiling tile is employed here as a magnetic knife rack.

When it came to designing the interior, another important aspect was to ensure that we allowed an abundance of surfaces to display art. One solution has been to install plenty of shelving, both wall-mounted and more flexible shelves on wheels, such as industrial-looking work-in-progress trolleys and wood and steel trolleys rescued from defunct shoe factories. The wall-mounted shelves found throughout the house come in a variety of shapes and sizes. Mark's favourite new design are the brackets that hold our kitchen shelves – thin stainless-steel supports, folded like a simple origami mountain fold. Stainless steel shelves also hold our collection of wooden vessels by Ray Key. The man-made and natural materials are contrasting, yet there is an intriguing similarity, too.

Art is even found in the kitchen, where we've installed a concrete shelf that runs the length of the room and almost appears to float, despite its reassuring solidity. It provides a surface for, among other things, Ethiopian cooking vessels that resemble wonky over-sized coffee mugs, delicate hand-blown glass, rustic stoneware and a pair of vintage exercise pins.

The house is full of unexpected touches too, such as a fire surround that was created from pieces of an intricately carved Indian doorframe. This has had a few holes drilled along the top that are now the perfect home for fragrant, smouldering incense sticks. Strings of ethnic jewellery hang next to the fireplace, adjacent to a row of carved Ethiopian paddles, which look a little like oversized wooden spoons. Another cluster of Ray Key's hand-turned wooden vessels sit alongside pieces of wooden fruit and vintage folding rulers. These displays reveal that even the most unlikely objects can make happy bedfellows and prove that you don't have to be precious about how you display art.

OPPOSITE ABOVE LEFT This door has had its layers of paint peeled back, leaving behind a patchy, rough texture that stands out from the crowd.

OPPOSITE ABOVE RIGHT An old wooden shoe trolley is home to a collection of teapots, including classic Brown Betties, a shiny enamel teapot and an oriental-shaped modern glass teapot, perfect for the bright colours of herbal and fruit teas. Large print block and old metal shop front letters spell out the ever-comforting word.

OPPOSITE BELOW A thin steel shelving unit holds an artful display of delicate wooden vessels by Ray Key, with wooden folded rulers and old wooden apples alongside.

Q&A (answered by Mark)

What are you working on at the moment?
Finishing this house although, rather like our farmhouse, I'm sure it will be constantly evolving so probably it will never be quite finished! We're also curating a pop-up show during Hay festival fortnight – an exhibition of I-D magazine covers between 1980– 2010. It's our first event in our gallery, so it's quite exciting and just a little bit nerve racking.

How do you relax?
By putting my feet up on one of our extra-large loft sofas and listening to my current favourite CD of a 1950's recording of Spanish classical guitarist Andres Segovia with pen and paper close to hand.

Who is your favourite artist/designer?
The architect Zaha Hadid – her buildings are monumental. I'm looking forward to seeing the finished London Aquatic Centre that she is designing for the 2012 Olympic games.

LONDON TERRACE

Artist Kate Blee's remodelled Victorian terraced home in London

KATE BLEE IS AN ARTIST WORKING PREDOMINANTLY WITH TEXTILES. HER WORK IS A ROBUST EXPLORATION OF COLOUR RELATIONSHIPS AND DIFFERENT TEXTURES AND ENCOMPASSES SPONTANEOUS BURSTS OF COLOUR PAINTED DIRECTLY ON TO FABRIC THAT SHE HAS PREVIOUSLY DYED TO HER EXACT REQUIREMENTS. KATE HAS WORKED WITH MANY FAMOUS NAMES INCLUDING SIR PAUL SMITH, JIM THOMPSON AND DONNA KARAN. HER WORK APPEARS IN PUBLIC COLLECTIONS RANGING FROM THE VICTORIA AND ALBERT MUSEUM TO THE CRAFTS COUNCIL.

THIS PAGE A bright cherry-red bench, designed by Kate Blee's architect husband Charles Thomson, brightens up an alcove in the open-plan kitchen/dining space and provides a vantage point for Maisie, one of the family cats. The table is an elegant Ercol design; its slim legs and tabletop chime with the slender bench. The chairs are by Finnish designer Alvar Aalto.

OPPOSITE One of Kate's abstract paintings makes a dramatic statement on a white wall and is in sharp contrast to the well-worn Stockman tailors' dummy, which was found in Portobello market, and the tiny chair, saved by Kate from her childhood.

LEFT A flip-top window seat cunningly doubles as extra storage. Its moulded modern shape contrasts perfectly with the natural wood and basket bowls from Uganda.

BELOW LEFT A large painting – 'Circle', by Kate Blee – leads on to the bathroom.

RIGHT A bright Cappellini red cross cabinet hangs above the roll-top bath, adding a splash of primary colour to the otherwise monochrome bathroom. The edge of a 1950's Danish chair can just be seen peeking out from behind the door.

FAR RIGHT A large canvas by Kate entitled 'Untitled Map' fills the wall in this corner of the house. The 'Sussex University' chair was designed by Basil Spence. A painting by Sarah Blee sits on top of two stacked chests.

The simple graphic statements made by Kate's work are reflected in the sleek lines of her home. Once through the front door, you would be hard pressed to know that you were in a traditional Victorian terraced house, thanks to the clever remodelling of the space by Kate's architect husband Charles Thomson.

Charles' brief for the design was to create a flexible home with the ability to adapt to the requirements of both the family and of work; to establish a space where things could easily be moved

around and added or subtracted to whenever necessary. All vital ingredients when you work from home and have three children! Thanks to Charles, the result is a cool and minimal yet family-friendly home with a ground floor that encompasses Kate's studio and an open-plan living space.

The house is full of clever storage solutions, including a flip-top resin window seat in the kitchen, flanked by slim shelves full of well-thumbed cookbooks. In another room the bookshelves, filled with tomes on art and architecture, can be hidden from view by smooth sliding doors. In Kate's studio there are shelves filled with neatly labelled files of former projects and notes on current work. She has cleverly turned an extra-large stretched canvas to the wall and uses the wooden supports as narrow shelves that hold rows of her abstract paintings and colour experimentations.

This elegant house is the perfect backdrop for Kate's artworks as well as pieces by members of the extended family and Kate's

sons. There are brightly painted canvases illuminating darker corners and paintings in more muted colours where the light is stronger. Kate's painted cashmere scarves and fabrics hang loosely from hooks on the walls or are casually draped around vintage dressmakers' dummies, giving an idea of how the patterns will change and interact with the light when worn.

Kate's textiles soften the harder edges of the house. The smooth floors are broken up with the hand-woven kilims Kate has created in collaboration with renowned rug maker Christopher Farr and provide warmth and comfort for bare feet. Even the work-

in-progress textiles hanging up to dry from suspended wires feel like a vital part of the house. It is an important feature of the handmade home that the art is used alongside everyday items, and in Kate's house this is certainly the case. Melin Tregwynt blankets custom-made especially for Kate protect the sofas from jammy fingers rather than being neatly folded away in a display cabinet, and contemporary designer furniture from the 1970s onwards collected by Charles is used by all the family.

The furniture is in keeping with the clean lines of the house. Spindly-legged blonde wooden chairs, stools and tables lend

a Scandinavian feel. The modernist aesthetic is deliberately broken up with the addition of vintage family items, including a well-travelled, slightly battered trunk, frayed tailors' dummies and Kate's favourite childhood chair.

The walls in this home are simply painted in tones of white so they don't fight with the vibrant colours of Kate's work. The modern extension is painted in dark greys for a grittier feel. However, the home is brightened up by confident bursts of red throughout, often in the form of Kate's artworks. The result is a cheerful home that works as both a studio and a place for the whole family to gather together at the end of the day, surrounded by art but not intimidated by it.

OPPOSITE ABOVE LEFT
A large stretched canvas has been turned to face the wall in Charles Thomson's well-organized studio area. Its wooden frame holds a series of paintings by Kate. The red Hans Wegner chair was inherited. The table is a simple Alvar Aalto design.
OPPOSITE ABOVE RIGHT
A canvas by Perry Roberts hangs above an original Mogensen sofa. The 'Cross' cushion is by Kate as are the scarves hanging to the left. The coffee table is by Kate's talented son, Finn Thomson.
LEFT Tallulah and Maisie, the family cats.
RIGHT A bentwood rocking chair by Michael Thonet is lit by a counter-balanced reading lamp.

RIGHT Folded pieces of work in progress, painted by hand in deep, inky blue stripes.

FAR RIGHT Some of Kate's well-used brushes hanging to dry.

BELOW Kate's workspace shows the importance of being well organized.

OPPOSITE A group of Kate's hand-painted linens hang in the light-filled space that links the new and old parts of the house. The two small stools are from Uganda and the woven fishing basket is from Thailand.

Q&A

Which is your favourite room in your house?

I love the whole house. It's always on the move – none of the spaces are completely fixed, and we move things around and take away and add things. The rooms are fluid multi-functional spaces, which reflect the way we use the house for both living and working.

Vintage or modern, and why?

Both. Most of the things we have in the house we are personally connected to in some way. Either they belonged to family members or we have collected them (my husband Charles Thomson has always collected contemporary furniture) or they have been made by our son Finn, who has made us a table and a chair. The art in the house is my work, work by our sons, my sister- and brother-in-law, who are both artists, our friends and my grandfather.

Where do you get your best ideas?

All over the place and at any time. In the nicest possible way, I'm always at work!

What is your top travel destination?

Wherever my family or friends are.

BELOW LEFT A large handmade wooden bowl full of misty purple plums sits on a well-worn, beautifully textured table.

BELOW CENTRE A collection of hand-crafted thumbsticks, in a variety of woods and different lengths, means there's a stick for every visitor. They lean casually on scuffed white-painted wooden boards next to the door, which boasts a traditional smithy-made thumb latch.

BELOW RIGHT This traditionally shaped wooden spoon rack was made by Dorian after many hours spent studying the Welsh vernacular designs at St Fagans National History Museum, near Cardiff. This simple design hangs on the whitewashed stone wall in the kitchen and holds an attractive collection of handcrafted wooden spoons.

OPPOSITE A shiny, bright red Rayburn range cooker provides a cheerful splash of glossy colour among the more natural colours and textures of the cottage kitchen. In this traditional Welsh stone cottage, the range has its work cut out – not only is it required for cooking, but it also has the all-important job of providing much-needed warmth throughout the house. A piece of rough unhemmed linen drying on the polished rail serves as a simple but effective tea towel.

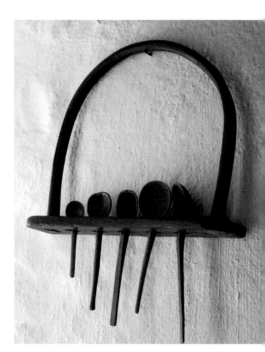

WELSH RETREAT

Translated from the Welsh, the name of this tiny cottage means Clear Hill

THIS COTTAGE HIDDEN AWAY IN THE CARMARTHENSHIRE COUNTRYSIDE HAS A REASSURINGLY PLAIN AND SIMPLE INTERIOR, BUT A FEW MODERN TOUCHES ENSURE THAT IT IS A COMFORTABLE BOLTHOLE FOR ANYONE WISHING TO ESCAPE THE CITY AND THE NOISY DISTRACTIONS OF MODERN LIFE. THERE IS MANY A SPOT TO CURL UP WITH A NOVEL, WRAPPED IN A COSY WELSH BLANKET AND ENJOYING A COUPLE OF WELSH CAKES WARMED ON THE BRIGHT RED RAYBURN.

BELOW A traditional cooking range sits in the inglenook fireplace. There is an unusual adjustable chimney sway hanging above that would have been used for holding cooking pots above the fire. A wooden candlebox hangs on the wall above the stove and nearby there is a copper warming pan, which could still play an important role in the winter months, though hot-water bottles seem easier somehow! A handmade stickback chair provides extra seating around the stove. **OPPOSITE** A built-in settle works as a screen and room divider. Next to it, another group of wooden thumbsticks await keen walkers, as does the pair of green wellies. Skeins of undyed wool hangs from pegs in the entrance, providing a softer texture that tempers the hardness of the other surfaces: wood, painted brick and traditional Welsh slate.

This Carmarthenshire retreat is one of a pair of smallholders' cottages, known as *tyddyn* in Welsh, which have been brought carefully back to life by the owner, London-based but Welsh-born chartered building surveyor Dorian Bowen. When Dorian discovered Bryn Eglur, the 17th-century cottage – made up of a kitchen and parlour downstairs, two interconnecting bedrooms upstairs and an attached barn – had been empty for at least forty years. It was in desperate need of repair and was fortunate to be taken on by Dorian, who grew up about a mile away on his parent's farm. He had long been fascinated with the idea of bringing an abandoned building back to its former glory – a glory centred around the charms of rustic simplicity – exactly what Dorian yearned for after years in London.

The windows and doors of the cottage had rotted away and so had many of the beams and trusses supporting the structure. Together with a team of local builders, Dorian undertook the role of reconstructing and, wherever possible, repairing the cottage using local materials. In fact much of the wood in the cottage came from a nearby forest belonging to Dorian's parents.

A combination of childhood memories of visits to old cottages and farmhouses and many hours of research at St Fagans National History Museum near Cardiff, enabled Dorian to repair and furnish

Bryn Eglur in a traditional Welsh vernacular style, taking the cottage back to a time when everything was made by hand simply because there was no other option. Today many of these skills have been forgotten, but in his restoration of the cottage Dorian has taken the time and trouble to bring them back to life, too.

The former kitchen has an impressive inglenook fireplace. Traditionally, such fireplaces had chimneys made from woven hazel, which may sound a bit of a a health and safety hazard, but which was just the thing for the smouldering peat fires of the past. In Dorian's cottage the hazel had long since rotted away, but rather than replacing it with a modern alternative Dorian cut new

hazel sticks from a nearby hedge, taught himself how to weave and rebuilt the chimney in the traditional fashion.

The new kitchen, once a cowshed and attached to the rest of the home by a long hallway, is filled with light and space. It has a beautiful slate hearth that was found beneath a rusty Victorian grate and oven. The kitchen boasts a few modern touches; there is something to be said for the ease of switching on an oven rather than chopping wood to light a fire and boil water!

The cottage is simply furnished with antique Welsh pieces or objects made by Dorian and based on his research at St Fagans. The larger of the two bedrooms has a vintage wrought-iron bed

ABOVE LEFT The dishes draining in the slate sink are all handmade, including a salt-glazed pot, a wooden breadboard and a couple of marble bowls.

ABOVE A dark-wood traditional Welsh dresser holds a mixture of pewter platters and wooden plates, ladles and bowls, both new and old.

piled with Welsh blankets. The other, smaller bedroom is home to a traditional timber box-bed sourced from a local rectory and brightened up by a hand-stitched patchwork quilt from the 1930s.

At Bryn Eglur, the handmade elements are integral to the functionality of the cottage. Everything is intended for use, just as it was in the past, including traditional spoon racks, stoneware bowls, Welsh blankets and stickback chairs. These chairs were once made by 'bodgers' or wood turners in the Carmarthen and Cardigan area. Dorian discovered that they were becoming increasingly rare and taught himself to make them based on 17th-century examples at St Fagans. Dorian can often be found scouring local woodland for the perfect curved branch – like everything in the cottage, his dedication is well worth the effort.

OPPOSITE BELOW An old farmhouse table with a well-scrubbed top, bleached to a pleasing paleness over the years, is laid with a simple lunch of bread and cheese. A mixture of old wooden chairs provides plenty of seating for incoming diners.
THIS PAGE The painting above the Welsh slate fireplace is by Sir Kyffin Williams.

THIS PAGE Here the wooden walls have been painted in a welcoming bright green, contrasting with the other, more natural shades. The scuffed tones of the boards are picked up by the waffle blanket. Further quilts and blankets sit outside the bedroom on an old wooden bench. The fixed ladder leads rather precariously up to the loft. **RIGHT** Ty Unnos (the one-night house), quietly showing off its simple, thatched beauty.

RIGHT A well-worn wooden staircase leads up to the cosy bedrooms.

BELOW RIGHT A traditional timber box-bed provides a cosy nest in this bedroom. They were often to be found placed back to back in Welsh parlours in the 18th century, creating snug little rooms within rooms when space and a good nights sleep were at a premium. The patchwork dates from the 1930s.

Q&A

What is your favourite thing about Bryn Eglur?

Rural seclusion. Kipling describing his home said: 'the house stands like a beautiful cup, on a saucer to match'. I think I've found my 'cup and saucer'.

Which materials do you most like to work with?

Anything sustainable that has a low impact on our environment but especially old wood, which improves with age. Something which has struck a chord with me during this project is the fact that you can 'be the change you want to see in the world' whether you are a 'minority of one or a majority of millions'.

What are you working on at the moment?

I'm currently working on an authentic reconstruction of the Ty Unnos (One-night house) – a legendary house built in a night between sunset and sunrise. This has been an extraordinary journey and what makes it even more interesting is the fact that I've relived the experience of constructing my own 'homemade' home, which has provided a compelling insight into Welsh cottage life.

THIS PAGE Even the cat plays an integral role in this muted colour scheme. Warm grey walls blend with the heather-coloured linen of the corner sofa. The stripped floorboards are accented by one of Claudy's Drenthe Heath sheepskin rugs.

LEFT The family cat rests on one of Claudy Jongstra's pieces of densely textured felt. **RIGHT** Claudy's naturally dyed Drenthe Heath sheep's wool comes in a dramatic array of colours, from soft heathery pink to vibrant magenta. **BELOW** An undyed piece of shaggy wool looks as if it has come straight off the back of one of Claudy's flock. The cushions add brightness to the grey plaster and pigment walls.

DUTCH FARMHOUSE

A farmhouse filled with handwoven textiles from the owner's flock of sheep

THE HOME OF ACCLAIMED DUTCH TEXTILE ARTIST CLAUDY JONGSTRA IS A SMALL BUT WELL-TENDED FARM WITH ADJOINING WORKSHOPS IN SPANNUM, A VILLAGE IN THE NORTH OF THE NETHERLANDS. IT IS FILLED WITH HER FINISHED FELT ARTWORKS, BLANKETS AND WOOLLY RUGS AS WELL AS SCRAPS OF BRIGHTLY COLOURED WOOL LEFT OVER FROM HER ENDLESS EXPERIMENTATION WITH TEXTURE AND COLOUR. EACH PART OF CLAUDY'S WORKING PROCESSES SEEMS TO PRODUCE SOMETHING BEAUTIFUL AND WORTHY OF DISPLAY AND HER HOME IS A PRIME EXAMPLE OF THE PARED-BACK SIMPLICITY THAT'S NECESSARY TO SHOWCASE THESE TEXTURAL DELIGHTS.

BELOW LEFT A chiselled stone sink has a stripy edge thanks to the exaggerated tooling marks that show off its handmade quality. An extra-long wooden chopping board leaning against the white tiles is ideal for long French baguettes.

BELOW RIGHT The vintage wooden table with traditionally turned legs is in contrast to the very modern, simply designed stools. A sculptural basket made from wide pieces of woven birch wood sits on top of a rough and ready wooden cupboard. An extra long window allows plenty of daylight to flood into this relaxed dining space.

RIGHT Brightly coloured glazed tiles divide the kitchen space from the rest of the room. They add a splash of brightness in the face of the darkly painted kitchen cupboards. A noticeboard above the low wooden bench holds family photos.

Claudy originally trained as a fashion designer, but her imagination was fired after seeing a traditional Mongolian yurt with its colourful inlaid pattern on display in a museum. She soon mastered the traditional technique of felting and began to make fabrics in which wool was felted with silk fibres or combined with transparent silk organza. She has been continuously tinkering, experimenting and pushing the boundaries of felt-making ever since. Claudy's work has evolved from small domestic pieces to vast, sculptural installations that can be found in international collections that include the Victoria and Albert Museum in London and The Museum of Modern Art in New York. Her work has also been used in the collections of well-known fashion designers, such as Donna Karan and Christian Lacroix.

Claudy's work is impressive on a grand scale, but it is also a perfect balance of tradition and sustainability combined with contemporary aesthetics. She encourages awareness of the connection between the maker and the materials – a far cry from the disposable fabrics and

OPPOSITE ABOVE Designer chairs and stools sit around the simply shaped table, which was made for Claudy by artist friend Marc Mulders. The solid natural ash Z-shaped chair is the Zig Zag by Gerrit Rietveld, while the patchwork stool is by another Dutch designer maker, Piet Hein Eek. The large woollen rug is one of Claudy's own designs.

fashion favoured today. The sheep whose fleeces she transforms are the oldest breed in Western Europe. Claudy uses time-honoured handmade techniques such as carding and spinning to produce the wool, which she then dyes using traditional dyes made from madder, St John's wort and dried African marigolds. These natural dyes produce amazingly vibrant colours, from golden yellow and bright orange to deep corals that are much more intense than anything produced using synthetic dyes.

Claudy's home doubles as her workspace. A flock of Drenthe Heath sheep, with long hair and impressively curled horns, roam freely on her farmland and she has a special garden in which she grows the plants for her natural dyes. A neighbouring workshop serves as a dyeworks and is filled with huge steel pots bubbling over gas burners. The domestic areas of her home are filled with tactile surfaces and plenty of well-organized storage to keep children's toys, books and clothes under control.

LEFT Storage space has been cleverly built into Claudy's attic, using recycled wooden boards. BELOW LEFT The plywood chair with slim metal legs in the corner is the Jason chair by Carl Jacobs. RIGHT A sheepskin rug warms up the bathroom. OPPOSITE A bed has been built into the rafters, creating a cosy hideaway for Claudy's son.

The house is painted in tones of grey and white that alter in intensity as the light changes throughout the day. These muted colours are the perfect backdrop to Claudy's textiles, which fill the house. The pieces in her home are small-scale domestic versions in comparison to her huge installation works, but they have the same effect, softening any hard edges and bringing a spectrum of sunset colours into all the rooms. There are felt-covered cushions and generous piles of blankets on all the sofas or beds and almost every room boasts a long-haired rug that appear to have come directly off the backs of the sheep – except that some of them are bright egg-yolk yellow! They make you want to walk barefoot around the house and bury your toes in their long, unkempt strands. Claudy's work is incredibly tactile and cries out to be touched; something that Claudy is keen to encourage.

As well as textiles, the home is filled with the warm, honey tones of wood, especially on the upper floor. There is a mix of shiny contemporary pieces of wooden furniture alongside the more rustic traditional pieces you might expect of a Dutch farmhouse. A stool by fellow Dutch designer Piet Hein Eek was handmade using rescued wood that was patchworked together, resulting in surprising combinations of colour and texture. There is more salvaged wood to be found upstairs, where it has been used to create clever storage spaces and a nest-like child's bed built into the rafters by a local carpenter. Other pieces have been given by artist and designer friends or are collectable designer chairs with a simple elegance that is perfectly suited to Claudy's tactile home.

OPPOSITE A bank of cupboards have been built in this bedroom, making use of a difficult space. They hide a mass of children's toys, books and clothes. A vibrant oriental kite adds a flash of colour, along with the bright yellow rug, made by Claudy, and which offers a cosy contrast to the polished concrete floor.

LEFT Dried African marigolds are just some of the flowers used by Claudy to dye her wool.

BELOW The room set aside for the natural dyeing process has the feel of a mad scientist's laboratory, with over-sized metal pots, protruding rubber pipes and experimental dyeing notes scribbled on pieces of paper and pinned to the wall. It is a room where magic happens.

Q&A

What is your favourite thing about your home?
The kitchen table, which was especially handmade for us by our friend the Dutch artist, Marc Mulders. It's the perfect place to enjoy dinner and drinks with family and/or friends long into the evening.

What materials do you like to work with?
Wool spun by hand from our flock of Drenthe Heath sheep.

What is your favourite colour combination?
At the moment it is a beautiful golden mixture, which you get when you blend rhubarb root with St John's wort and cochineal…it is amazing.

Who is your favourite artist/designer?
Gerrit Rietveld – a Dutch architect and furniture designer. He is probably best known for his Schroder house in Utrecht, which is like a vast Mondrian painting brought to life in 3 dimensions, and his Zig Zag chair.

How do you relax?
Looking after our bees – they help pollinate the hortus botanicus where historic varieties of dye-plants grow.

DUTCH BARN
The home of a dynamic design duo

INA MEIJER AND MATTHIJS VAN CRUIJEN ARE THE PARTNERSHIP BEHIND MULTI-DISCIPLINARY DESIGN TEAM STUDIO INAMATT. THEIR HOME, WHICH ENCOMPASSES THEIR STUDIO, IS TO BE FOUND IN A VAST AGRICULTURAL BARN IN THE VILLAGE OF PINGJUM IN THE NORTHERN NETHERLANDS, THE CONVERSION AND INTERIOR OF WHICH THEY DESIGNED THEMSELVES. SUCH BARNS ARE TO BE FOUND DOTTED THROUGHOUT THE LANDSCAPE OF THE AREA, BUT THERE CAN'T BE MANY THAT HAVE SUCH A SLEEK YET INFORMAL INTERIOR.

THIS PAGE AND OPPOSTE The acid brights of the sofa and the patterned cushions liven up the otherwise neutral living space, but don't be fooled by the room's simplicity. Behind the sofa a very grown-up flower press creates an unusual work of art alongside more traditional artworks by Annemiek de Beer and the enormous portrait just peeking in on the right, by Katinka Lampe. The painting on the far left is by Andrea Letterie.

In their design practice, Ina and Matt work together on a diverse range of projects, from mood/colour boards, creative shop and restaurant interiors, products and architecture – the list goes on and on. What links the work is its playfulness and imagination. An example of this can be seen on the rugs they designed for a hotel based on Rorschach tests – ink blots on a super-sized woolly scale. They are a couple who clearly love what they do and enjoy working together. This follows through into their home, which is light and airy, thanks to the open-plan layout and enormous windows. The atmosphere is bright, breezy and informal.

The bones of the barn conversion echo the clean lines and geometric shapes found in much of Ina and Matt's work. The floor is one huge expanse of scrubbed concrete, surrounded by a mix of simply painted white walls and walls clad in reclaimed wooden boards. The barn is reinforced by a series of wooden supports mounted on raw concrete plinths. The natural palette is the ideal backdrop to their collection of paintings and handmade textiles and the quirky array of mismatched chairs and other furniture. Everything feels 'off the peg', like nothing you have ever seen before. One end of the living space contains a simple table

surrounded by a variety of mismatched chairs in all manner of shapes and sizes, most of which are prototypes – Ina and Matt have many designer friends, which means they are lucky enough to be able to fill their home with many designer donations. The same goes for the diverse collection of artworks. These are simply propped up on the pre-cast concrete shelf that runs the full length of the living space, allowing Matt and Ina to reshuffle their displays whenever the fancy takes them, or if they acquire a new piece.

The living area is large and high-ceilinged but still manages to be cosy at the same time. Much of this is down to the cheery lemon-yellow sofa, piled with an array of gloriously patterned cushions. Other areas in this space include a group of friendly

LEFT A simple wooden table is surrounded by a group of mismatched chairs, including some by young Dutch furniture designer Wannes Royaards and a vintage Eames chair. The lampshade, which hangs down from the rafters on a long piece of flex, is porcelain and designed by Dick van Hoff, while the tall, skinny, slightly industrial-looking floor lamp is the Toio lamp by Achille Castiglioni. The softly toned floral painting is by Annemiek de Beer.
ABOVE RIGHT A sneaky peek of Ina and Matt's studio pinboard.
RIGHT A group of vintage 1950's bamboo chairs sit in a companionable huddle around the traditional wood-burning stove.

OPPOSITE ABOVE A wall covered in clean white tiles partially divides the kitchen space from the rest of the open-plan ground floor. A neatly designed recess holds shelves made from thick wooden boards – a much-needed natural material among the glossy tiles and sleek stainless-steel appliances.

curvy chairs gathered around an impressive wood-burning stove. The efficiently designed kitchen is cleverly separated from the rest of the open-plan ground floor by way of being raised slightly on a neat platform. The kitchen space is tiled from floor to ceiling with shiny white ceramic tiles, as is the block-shaped island that sits in the centre of the space and is home to both the oven and hob. The clean white tiles contrast with the bleached wood panelled wall, which hides a bank of built-in cupboards. This wooden wall divides the kitchen from the creative hub that is the studio. Here, ideas and images are pinned haphazardly onto

ABOVE The sleeping areas in Ina and Matt's converted barn are divided up with neatly sewn pieces of canvas. These panels are simply suspended from the wooden rafters using lengths of thick string threaded through metal eyelets punched into the canvas.

LEFT A Moroccan Berber cloak makes for a glamorous bedspread in this bedroom behind a wall of canvas. The cloak has tiny mirrors sewn into the tufted stripes, which twinkle in the light.

OPPOSITE ABOVE Here, the canvas panels have been used to create storage space in the place where the rafters meet the walls. A neat sofa by Kho Liang Ie for Artifort is piled with striped quilts from Syria and pillows from Kashmir; the hare doll reclining next to them was made by Ina. The colourful floorcovering is a vintage Boucherouite rag rug from Morocco.

OPPOSITE BELOW Softly painted wooden doors, originally used as part of a colour collection for Ina and Matt's design consultancy work, now open into the upstairs rooms.

a wooden board, yet the overall effect is very visually appealing. This is a wonderful place to work, with its well-organized storage and the abundance of natural light and space.

The upper floor is home to the bedrooms and a bathroom fitted neatly into scrubbed wooden rafters that have been reinforced with unusual rounded beams which, with their tree-trunk-like beauty, create something of a log-cabin effect and are a testament to Matt and Ina's subtle attention to detail. The sleeping areas are divided up with large natural canvas panels, which are tied to the rafters using strong string threaded through extra large eyelets. The canvas walls add to the cosy yet outdoorsy feel of the upper floor – it makes sleeping at Ina and Matt's feel like a sophisticated and extremely comfortable version of camping! The canvas panels are also used to create useful storage in the awkward space where the sloping ceiling meets the walls.

RIGHT A pair of vintage cabinets have been humorously painted in his 'n' hers shades of pink and blue.
FAR RIGHT A dress made by Ina for the Raad van State in The Hague (the high court of the Netherlands) creates a shadowy silhouette behind a canvas panel.
BELOW Ina and Matt's cat stretches out on their bed. A Jieldé floor lamp is angled over the bed while a small round window allows a little natural light into the room.

The beds are covered with coloured throws, blankets and bedspreads – nothing too distracting, to ensure that a good night's sleep is had by all. The bathroom is similarly minimal, with a free-standing bath on unadorned feet, piles of towels and a cheerful rubber duck for company. This sums up the entire feel of Ina and Matt's home – it is fun and friendly, filled with an atmosphere of creativity, yet at the same time it is considered and minimal – a barn conversion in the Dutch meadows without a trace of twee.

Q&A

Who is your favourite artist/designer?
Matt: David Hockney, Michel Gondry.
Ina: Rachel Whiteread, Vita Sackville West.
What is your favourite thing about your house?
The colour in the light of the house, and the landscape surrounding it.
Where do you get your best ideas?
In the garden.
Where is your top travel destination?
Anywhere in my mind.

THIS PAGE The lofty bathroom is kept simple, with a roll-top bath standing on unadorned metal feet. A round wooden pole, which is an extra support for the rafters, doubles up as a hanging space for clothes and towels.

THIS PAGE The kitchen dining space is simply furnished with elegant white chairs around a table made from a couple of abandoned doors. The moulding process, known as shuttering, has imprinted the knots and grain from the wood into the concrete walls. A narrow strip of glass has been fitted high into the gable-end wall.

LEFT A sourdough loaf sits on the sleek white worksurface, providing a textural contrast. **RIGHT** The outside space continues the concrete and glass theme. An almost mirror image has been created externally, which gives the concrete beam the ability to appear as if it is floating. **BELOW** A traditional stickback wooden chair holds a precarious looking pile of cushions covered in Welsh wool from Damson and Slate.

MODERN RUSTIC

A rural Welsh cottage with a surprisingly modern interior

BRYNCYN LIES TEN MILES FROM BRYN EGLUR, DORIAN BOWEN'S OTHER RURAL RETREAT, YET THEY ARE A MILLION MILES APART IN TERMS OF INTERIOR DESIGN. THIS SIMPLE WHITEWASHED STONE COTTAGE IS SET IN THE TINY VILLAGE OF TANGLWYST WITH STUNNING VIEWS OF THE PRESELI MOUNTAINS. THROWING OPEN THE FRONT DOOR OF THE COTTAGE REVEALS THE SURPRISE WITHIN: A LIGHT AND AIRY OPEN-PLAN INTERIOR. THE FORMER TWO-UP, TWO-DOWN COTTAGE AND COWSHED HAS BEEN OPENED UP INTO ONE LARGE SPACE WITH A CONTEMPORARY FIREPLACE LEADING ONTO AN EQUALLY UNEXPECTED MODERNIST OUTSIDE SPACE COMPLETE WITH CEDAR HOT TUB.

LEFT A sliding glass door spans the entire length of the kitchen wall, allowing a view out into the stunningly rugged Welsh landscape and showing why everything has been kept so minimal and simple – so as not to compete with the amazing view.

THIS PAGE This picture shows the stunning architectural design that has been bolted onto a traditional Welsh cottage. The large pond brings a softer feel to the shuttered concrete exterior.

The cottage, accessed down a bumpy track, offers rustic tranquillity with a breathtakingly modern twist. In less capable hands this paradox might jar, but here it works thanks to Dorian's scrupulous attention to the smallest details.

When Dorian found this cottage he was uninspired by its Victorian details. He sensed the opportunity to create something entirely different and, with the words of the master of minimalism John Pawson ringing in his ears, he grasped it with both hands. Pawson recommends 'paring a building down until…you know you mustn't remove anything else', and this is what Dorian has done at Bryncyn. The cottage is a subtle combination of traditional and modern. Dorian hasn't removed every trace of the old interior but has left the significant details, and this is the key to the success of the conversion.

Some walls retain patches of plaster that have crumbled away to reveal the Welsh stone beneath. In the modernist setting, these areas take on the feeling of an abstract painting yet are also a gentle reminder of the origin and location of the cottage. On other walls the stone has not been smoothly plastered but instead just given a lick of white paint, lending the space a subtle sense of texture. One end of the room has a wall of bleached wooden boards, where a painting of Welsh cottages is casually propped.

LEFT A sleek modern wood-burning stove sits on top of a low slate table. Chopped logs are stored underneath. A remnant from the past, a little alcove in the stone wall, holds books for fireside reading. **BELOW LEFT** A rough wooden door contrasts with the painted staircase. **RIGHT** A pair of traditional stickback chairs nestle together in front of a stone and plaster wall.

The large open space leads to a stunning extension in the former cowshed, where Dorian has made the most of modern materials such as concrete and glass. However, even here Dorian has retained a link with the past: an original Welsh slate step, worn with years of use, connects the kitchen and living space – an interesting detail from the old interior that was just too good to remove.

The walls in the kitchen/dining area look like they are made of horizontally laid wooden boards, but on closer inspection are revealed to be shuttered concrete. Again, the care and attention that Dorian puts into his conversions is evident. Working with his civil engineer brother, they spent hours experimenting to discover exactly the right wood to use for the shuttering – which would leave the best traces of the naturally knotty texture? Even after they found their answer, the concrete was sandblasted to create extra texture once the wood was removed. To allow a glimpse of the skyline beyond the cottage, Dorian inserted a strip window at the top of the concrete wall. The visual experience is also enhanced by a sliding glass door that stretches the width of the kitchen. The theme of concrete and glass continues onto the terrace, seamlessly linking inside and out.

Both the kitchen and living space are simply but effectively furnished. The kitchen chairs are white, while the table is made from a couple of doors,

OPPOSITE The living space in Bryncyn is sparsely furnished in a minimal style so the details are extra important. For the seating, Dorian has chosen a classic Mies van der Rohe Barcelona chair in white and an angular wooden sofa, which has echoes of a more traditional upright wooden settle.

merged together. In the living space there is a white Mies van der Rohe chair, an upholstered settle and an angular sofa. For warmth the space relies on a modern wood-burning stove on a low slate table.

A wooden ladder originally linked the two floors of the cottage but Dorian has installed a wooden staircase up to the main bedroom. This room reveals the bare bones of the building, with limewashed walls and an open ceiling. There are waffle blankets on the bed but the roof has been insulated using environmentally friendly sheep's wool so it isn't too chilly. The other bedroom can only be accessed via the original steep fixed ladder, so is not for the faint hearted!

Bryncyn is a testament to Dorian's creativity and his willingness to experiment both with materials and style.

OPPOSITE A daybed has been covered with an indigo blanket for added comfort in this corner of the cottage, while a similarly toned blanket with a bright yellow stitched edge is provided for extra warmth. All of this softens the feel of the rough stone wall.

ABOVE RIGHT The exposed stone wall is a reminder of the cottage's humble origins and provides a bit of rustic personality, which is added to by the hanging plumber's beads and hunk of olive oil soap.

BELOW RIGHT Bleached wooden boards create a cosy alcove.

Q&A

Handmade or mass produced?
Both have their inherent uses in design, although I have a preference towards handmade because of its uniqueness. However, I also use mass-produced items for practical reasons.

What materials do you most like to work with?
Glass and shuttered concrete, because it gives you amazing abilities to break with traditional forms of construction.

Where do you get your best ideas?
From magazines and the internet.

Who is your favourite artist/designer?
The architect John Pawson.

YUKO IS A FREELANCE FOOD STYLIST AND COOKERY BOOK WRITER LIVING AND WORKING IN TOKYO. AS IS OFTEN THE CASE WITH TOKYO LIVING, HER APARTMENT IS VERY SMALL. HOWEVER, THANKS TO YUKO'S INNATE SENSE OF STYLE AND THE EXTREMELY WELL-ORGANIZED STORAGE, THE BRIGHT LITTLE APARTMENT FEELS WELCOMING AND SURPRISINGLY SPACIOUS. IT IS REPLETE WITH CLEAN LINES THAT LEND A COOL GRAPHIC EDGE AND GIVE A RESTRAINED MINIMALIST APPEAL; NOT UNLIKE A MONDRIAN PAINTING, IF MONDRIAN HAD SWAPPED HIS PRIMARY COLOUR PALETTE FOR SHADES OF CREAM, BROWN AND WHITE!

TOKYO SPACE

A clever, compact Tokyo apartment

ABOVE & RIGHT As a cookery writer and food stylist, Yuko has a massive array of plates, dishes and noodle bowls, stacked in precarious-looking piles on all the available shelf space in her small kitchen. She also has a surprising amount of teapots, too.
OPPOSITE A couple of classic Hans Wegner Wishbone chairs provide a European element to the minimally furnished dining arrangements.

Yuko has been living in the apartment for eight years, yet in this relatively short time she has stamped her personality on the place. When she first acquired it, the apartment was in much need of renovation, which Yuko devised herself. One of the most important requirements was the need for well-considered storage, and plenty of it. Thus the apartment boasts many cupboards built deep into the walls and they are all uniformly finished with beautiful dark wooden doors with extra narrow horizontal slats. These handmade louvred doors have a textural quality that gives added interest to the space. Yuko made sure that all the available space was used, so the geometric-looking

BELOW An angular Ercol stacking chair, originally designed in 1957, sits at one side of the room. A simple piece of undyed natural linen divides two areas of the open-plan living space, creating shadows as it moves in the breeze. **RIGHT** A low-level desk holds bedtime reading while a metal desk lamp provides the necessary illumination. The tones in the bedroom are kept neutral to create a necessarily restful atmosphere. **OPPOSITE BELOW** A comfortable looking armchair upholstered in powder-blue linen lines up next to another classic Ercol stacking chair. Behind them are generous storage cupboards – vitally important in a small apartment.

cupboards have been installed from floor to ceiling. In places, the space has been divided with simple sheets of undyed linen suspended from the ceiling. These textiles soften the feel of the apartment, and give a more relaxed and feminine atmosphere. In a similar vein Yuko has hung a sheet of white linen behind her bed, softening the angular wooden bed frame.

The colour palette is one of soft neutrals with warmish tones. This adds a brightness that contrasts with the dark wooden floors and is unfussy and simple. Small injections of colour, mostly in shades of blue, are to be found in a sharply upholstered armchair, in the narrow pinstripes of a soft woollen blanket or along the edge of a pillow. The overall effect is one of a simple, refined and almost Zen-like Japanese minimalism. However, there is also a European influence. Frilly French fluted glass lampshades are suspended from the ceiling with lengths of clean white flex in the kitchen/dining space and living space. Sleek Ercol chairs sit in various quiet corners and there is a group of sculptural Hans Wegner Wishbone chairs gathered around the dining table, which is especially long – the ideal size for lots of guests who wish to sample Yuko's well-developed cooking skills.

The main focus of the apartment is one of entertaining, involving plenty of friends and even more food. The kitchen is testament to this. Every inch of cupboard space groans under the weight of pile upon pile of plates, bowls, glasses, cups and more plates, not to mention Yuko's collection of teapots. This is where the restraint so evident in the rest of the apartment comes to an end, but it speaks volumes of Yuko's passion for her work.

RIGHT A single twiggy stem has been placed in a vintage milk bottle on a clean white shelf, behind which a delicate handmade ceramic lotus flower leans against the pale wall. Light is reflected onto the still life by a small vintage mirror hung on the wall.

Q&A

What are you working on right now?
Currently I'm creating new recipes for Muji. In all of them I have to make use of their new clay cooking pot. I'm also doing the food styling for a Japanese snack company called Meiji Seika. All of this is alongside my usual work, which includes writing recipes for newspapers and magazines, working on a range of cookbooks and developing new food products…I'm pretty busy all the time!

What's in your fridge?
Nori seaweed, Jako (a small fish similar to sprats or anchovies and best eaten with rice), umeboshi (pickled plums), various vegetables, and jars of seasonings. I have four shelves in the refrigerator, but try to keep two just for work. I actually don't keep that much food in the refrigerator, so it is never that full.

What are your store-cupboard essentials?
They must be big cupboards with enough depth!

What is your favourite thing about your home?
Relaxing on the sofa in the living room.

THIS PAGE Yumiko changes the linen tablecloths every few days, delving into the huge collection of linens she has built up over years of running Fog Linen Work. **OPPOSITE ABOVE RIGHT** A simple hand-drawn calendar is pinned to the wall with a shiny little folding clip. **OPPOSITE BELOW RIGHT** A glazed jug holds a small bunch of colourful flowers. **OPPOSITE FAR RIGHT** The open shelves hold stacks of wonkily handmade ceramics, some made by two of Yumiko's favourite designers, Sherry Olsen and Diana Fayt.

JAPANESE MODERN

The beautifully simple Tokyo home of Fog Linen Work founder Yumiko Sekine

YUMIKO'S COMPANY, THE DELIGHTFULLY NAMED FOG LINEN WORK, STARTED WHEN SHE REALIZED THERE WAS A GAP IN THE MARKET FOR AFFORDABLE, EVERYDAY HOUSEHOLD LINENS. SHE TRAVELLED FROM JAPAN TO LITHUANIA, WHERE SHE TRACKED DOWN SEVERAL LINEN PRODUCERS TO CREATE HER DESIGNS. ALMOST TWENTY YEARS LATER, THE RESULT IS HIGH-QUALITY STYLISH, UTILITARIAN LINENS FOR USE THROUGHOUT THE HOME.

LEFT A little cast iron teapot sits on a square of knitted linen, waiting for the tea to brew.
BELOW LEFT A bank of shelves make the most of the available space in this corner. They hold books and magazines, which Yumiko tries to edit ruthlessly to maintain order in her home.
RIGHT The simple kitchen units keep things neat and tidy in the kitchen area.

Yumiko regularly produces simply styled, quirky and covetable Fog Linen Work catalogues, including one where she asked various designers and friends to show her linens at work in their homes. The sense of style and fun found in these little books, as well as in her newly built Fog Linen Work store in Tokyo, is reflected in her small, yet perfectly formed city home.

The tidy kitchen, where Yumiko spends most of her time, is a clean and well-organized example of a typical Japanese kitchen. The units, which are made up of drawers, are unfussy but admittedly a little basic, Yumiko was not too keen on them to begin with, but she has learned to appreciate their undeniable practicality. She has also managed to give the kitchen personality with the addition of her textile collection. Yumiko changes the linen tablecloth every few days, as she says it is an easy way to alter the mood of the house. The kitchen is home to stacks of plates and bowls, many of which were handmade by friends. There are some by Sherry Olsen, who creates ceramics with soft washes of abstract pattern, and others by Diana Fayt, whose plates, bowls and vessels are patterned with linear flowers and stems that seem almost etched into the porcelain. These wobbly ceramic towers sit alongside piles of neatly folded linens, which add pattern as well as colour. The open shelves add to the sense of space, as the light flows around them freely.

THIS PAGE An upright bench made from maple wood provides seating in the living space, though Yumiko admits to being on the lookout for something more comfortable to stretch out on. The rug was bought in San Francisco on one of Yumiko's many trips abroad. A piece of undyed linen hangs on the wall behind the bench and brings an element of softness to the hard edges of the room.

Q&A

Is there anything you would change about your home?

I would like to change the closet.

What are you working on right now?

We just moved our office and store into a new space so I have been moving things around there. I'm also working on designing new fabrics for spring. There is always so much work to do!

Who is your favourite artist/designer?

Sherry Olsen, Mark Bailey and Lynn Beldner.

How do you relax?

By playing with my cat, I like to watch all of the *Star Wars* movies (when I have time). I also really like lying in bed reading books.

THIS PAGE The bed linen in the guest bedroom is from the Fog Linen Work collection. It shows how linen improves and softens with age. An angular Jieldé lamp sits on a chunky three-legged stool.

There are more open shelves in the living space. Yumiko loves books but tries hard to be ruthless about disposing of those she no longer needs. Such a disciplined approach is necessary in a small home, though it's not always easy. The living room sofa is an angular upholstered maple bench. It may look the part, but Yumiko admits it's not that comfortable. Luckily, help is at hand in the shape of an inviting linen-covered chair with angular wooden arms that's tucked away in a quiet, light-filled corner.

The bedrooms are simple and sparsely furnished. The guest room has a bed on wheels dressed with linen sheets from Yumiko's collection providing soft and warm bedding. Natural light is diffused through sheer curtains, which also helps to soften the space. In another part of the house Yumiko has made a beautiful curtain using rectangular remnants of different-sized sheer linens patchworked together. She is often to be found at the desk in her bedroom sewing and creating new uses for her hard-working linen collection.

Yumiko says her overall objective is to keep her home as simple as possible, and it seems she has achieved this goal. Her small house feels clean, fresh and full of light and space. Hers is a natural modern style. Everything is well ordered and in its place, yet Yumiko's favourite linens ensure her home is not austere or hard-edged.

ABOVE LEFT Yumiko has a huge collection of linen. Here it is shown neatly ironed and folded in an array of stripes, checks and herringbone, as well as the varying shades of undyed natural linen.

ABOVE RIGHT A handmade Japanese chair with dark wooden arms sits in a corner of the living space upholstered in a light brown nubby linen. The set of curvy-legged tables came from San Francisco.

RIGHT The spectacular home of Fred and Laura Ingrams is one of startling contrasts, with a steel-framed grain store erected in the 1980s sitting beside a 16th-century wooden barn and linked by an open-roofed frame. The buildings are surrounded by the flat Norfolk countryside and the resultant big skies.

BELOW A stoneware vase holds a generous bunch of yellow and green foliage, the colours of which are found in many of Fred's paintings. Further decoration has been added to the vase in the shape of an ethnic necklace draped around its belly. A couple of smaller ceramic pieces nestle together under the branches.

NORFOLK GRAIN STORE

An unlikely conversion of a 1980's steel-framed grain store into a modern home

THE INSPIRING HOME OF FRED AND LAURA INGRAMS PROVES THAT BEAUTY CAN COME IN THE MOST UNLIKELY OF FORMS. AFTER LEAVING LONDON FOR THE QUIET OF AN IDYLLIC TIMBER-FRAMED THATCHED FARMHOUSE IN NORFOLK, THE COUPLE REALIZED THE DEMANDS OF WORK, FAMILY, ART AND A SMALL COLLECTION OF CHICKENS MEANT THEY NEEDED MORE SPACE, LIGHT AND LAND. THEY SET OUT WITH A BARN CONVERSION IN MIND, BUT NOTHING MATCHED THEIR EXACTING REQUIREMENTS. EVENTUALLY, THEY DID FIND A BARN BUT IT WAS THE INTRIGUING NEIGHBOURING 1980'S BREEZEBLOCK, STEEL-FRAMED INDUSTRIAL GRAIN STORE THAT TOOK THEIR EYE…

THIS PAGE Fred's oil paintings, in hues of blue, yellow and green, hang on the walls of the entrance hall to the couple's home. The floor is tiled with large pieces of polished slate that reflect the light flooding in through the enormous windows.

BELOW LEFT Close to the front door, a traditional high-backed wooden settle with storage space in the seat provides the perfect spot for pulling on wellington boots. These are neatly lined up in a practical and well-ordered storage space – just the thing for long muddy walks in the countryside. Coats, caps and hats in sludgy country-gent colours are piled on top of each other on a row of hooks.

BELOW RIGHT An antique dark wooden corner cupboard makes a practical storage solution. Roomy and deep, it provides an abundance of shelf space for Laura and Fred's collection of plates, bowls, glasses and primitive-looking stoneware cooking pots. A trio of curvy white vintage teapots are displayed in a row on top of the cupboard – a good indicator of what's to be found inside.

This imaginative couple, with a shared background in the world of interiors magazines – Fred was an art director, while Laura was a stylist and decoration editor at *House & Garden* magazine – immediately saw the opportunity to create something new and modern from this ungainly structure. With the help of a visionary set of friendly architects, Fred and Laura oversaw the conversion from the vantage point of a small caravan parked in the grounds. Putting up with a few months of cramped conditions was more than worth it. Once the fabric of the grain store was removed (the breeze blocks were crushed to form the basis of the driveway) leaving behind the steel frame and metal span roof, the foundations were in place for a stunning and surprisingly beautiful family home.

The house is made of steel, wood and glass; an array of contrasting materials and textures. The timber-framed walls were heavily insulated, then clad on the outside with Siberian Larch. This is a strong, durable wood (often used in velodromes) which will more than withstand

ABOVE Large squishy sofas offer a place to relax. One is covered in a light grey linen, which works well with the darker grey slate floor, while the other has been draped in a light coloured knitted woollen throw. The ribs of this blanket echo the grooves of the upturned metal dolly tubs, which have each been given a wooden lid and put into use as curvy side tables.

frosty East Anglian winters, and will improve with age as it fades from brown to silvery grey. The decision was made to leave a six-metre open-roofed section between the grain store and the neighbouring barn in order to allow even more light into the home. The exterior of the house is made up of graphic, geometric shapes, dictated by the original framework and added to by the banks of enormous bespoke windows, which link the house with the Norfolk landscape. Inside, the house is a generous mixture of

natural materials, traditional and classical furniture as well as recycled industrial objects and a few more modern pieces.

As well as running a hugely successful graphic design business with Laura, Fred is also an extremely talented artist. His large canvases of nudes and country landscapes, painted using a bold palette, are integral to the interior of the house. Along with his inky sketches they hang on almost every wall of the ground floor or lean casually on tables and on the floor. They provide a crucial

THIS PAGE Just because the overall mood of the home is one of quiet minimalism, it doesn't mean that all of the furniture has to be austere and hard-edged. A curvaceous and ornately carved Hungarian bench offers a resting place at the bottom of a flight of slick wooden stairs. With its slightly scuffed ankles, the bench shows endearing signs of wear and tear. In keeping with the origin of the piece, long linen grain sacks with a central blue stripe, also from Hungary, are used as cushions.

OPPOSITE RIGHT AND LEFT Around the corner from the vintage bench is the industrial-style kitchen. The stainless-steel units echo the steel frame of the building. The French stoneware jars, piles of wooden chopping boards, the oversized wooden table and bench all prevent the industrial steel from feeling too brutal. The addition of large family photos tacked to the wall also helps soften the edges.

handmade element to the home, lending the atmosphere a warmth and playfulness in the face of what could otherwise feel a little austere. The walls have been coated in bright white paint and, on the ground floor grey slate has been used to seamlessly tile the entire space, reflecting back even more of the natural daylight that streams in through the huge windows. This combination is a clean, unfussy backdrop to Fred's artwork as well as the couple's collections of pottery bowls, jugs and vases, which rest on a modern wooden table in the double-height reception area. A couple of comfortable-looking leather armchairs provide an ideal vantage point to enjoy all the art and craft.

The large kitchen reflects the industrial history of the house. It is made up of free-standing, stainless steel units and a double-sized stove. A family-sized wooden table and benches provides natural contrast, as do a scattering of stoneware jugs, some of which are used to hold a dazzling array of old and new utensils.

Upstairs the bedrooms are fitted snugly into the metal rafters, with triangular windows providing pockets of light. The beds are covered in pale linens with an extra helping of indigo blankets piled on a wooden bench. In another room, there are industrial pieces on display, including an angular bedside lamp and a factory chair. A linen bedspread provides a touch of softness.

The home of Fred and Laura Ingrams, their son Blake and Midge the Patterdale terrier (not to mention the ever-expanding family of chickens) is an architectural delight, filled with light that emphasizes the unusual angles provided by the steel framework of their home, and is testament to the creativity of the couple and their willingness to see potential in the unlikeliest of starting points.

RIGHT A boxy old watchmaker's counter-balanced lamp provides extra illumination in the bedroom – the light bounces off the metallic finish of the painted wall. An old machinist's chair adds to the smattering of industrial furniture throughout. This always works well in a bedroom, as the soft folds of the bedlinen works to soften its hard-edged good looks.

LEFT The sturdy craftsmanship of a handmade poplar and ash ladder provides an unusual way to display a collection of monogrammed red and white antique French linens.

ABOVE Framed family photos, children's books and a collection of tiny pairs of baby shoes create an intimate still life on a painted wooden French shelf unit.

Q&A

Who is your favourite artist/designer?

This changes all the time, but at the moment it's Richard Diebenkorn. I particularly love his early 1960's paintings.

Is there anything you would change about your home?

Not really. Even if we had had a bigger budget when we were building, I think we would have spent it on the other buildings here and also on the garden. I would love to be able to restore the 16th-century barn next to the house.

What is your favourite colour combination?

Again, this changes, but I am using a lot of yellow and green in my paintings at the moment – perhaps it is because of the time of year (spring).

Where or when do you get your best ideas?

Just before I go to sleep.

THIS PAGE An old smock dyed indigo provided the starting point for the colour scheme in this simply furnished, restful bedroom. A few of the antique French linens have been dyed too. The chair is a traditional stickback chair. A collection of beads hanging on the wall decorates the room just as they would decorate the wearer and give the space a more feminine feel, as does the collection of teapots lined up on the window ledge.

THIS PAGE The canvas blocks hanging in a row on the wall behind the table were painted by Ulla to reflect the colour palette she has used throughout the house. The extra-long dining table is surrounded by white vintage Eames chairs and the Maarten Van Severen's 0.3 chairs in a matching shade of grey. Soft overhead illumination is provided by a Glo-Ball pendant shade by Jasper Morrison. The light birch floorboards come from timber from the forest just outside.

LEFT The last of the afternoon sun streams through the trees in the forest that surrounds Ulla's house.
RIGHT A huge pile of neatly chopped wood awaits the long, dark Finnish winter. In the meantime, the logs create a beautiful picture piled up in the dark timber framed store.
BELOW A trio of handmade glazed ceramic plates. The one in front looks as though it has been dip dyed.

FINNISH FOREST HOUSE

The serene home of Finnish designer Ulla Koskinen and her husband Simon Rantanen

ULLA KOSKINEN STUDIED TEXTILE AND CLOTHING DESIGN AT THE UNIVERSITY OF ART AND DESIGN IN HELSINKI. SHE HAS WORKED WITH MANY WELL-KNOWN FINNISH COMPANIES, INCLUDING MARIMEKKO. ULLA IS ALSO THE CREATIVE FORCE BEHIND THE WOODNOTES TEAM, WHO DESIGN AND MANUFACTURE PRODUCTS INSPIRED BY PAPER YARN. ULLA'S DESIGN PHILOSOPHY CAN BE SEEN IN HER BEAUTIFULLY DESIGNED YET SIMPLE HOME, CLAD IN DARK TIMBER FROM TREES FELLED FROM THE FOREST OUTSIDE. IN HER DESIGN WORK ULLA STRIVES FOR A SENSE OF HARMONY AND TO DESIGN INTERIORS THAT EXPRESS THE CHARACTER OF THE INHABITANTS.

This very personal house has been designed as a 'dream home' for both Ulla and her family, away from the demands of Helsinki city life, so it is not surprising that it feels so delightfully restful. Despite its humble beginnings as a prefabricated structure, the home is in step with the everyday needs and emotions of Ulla's family, thanks to her close attention to every detail.

The ground floor is dominated by enormous windows that flood the open-plan living space with soft natural daylight. This is vital in a country that has such few hours of daylight during the winter months, and is a treat for the senses during the long summer days. The huge sheets of glass also reconnect the house and its inhabitants with nature as they look out into the landscape beyond, filled with a Finnish forest of skinny trees and dark evergreens. In fact the timber used in the construction of the house, including the flooring and much of the newly built furniture, was made from the trees felled to clear the plot on which the house now stands.

Ulla's home is full of gently contrasting tactile textures that sit happily together. These textures add to the comforting nature of the house. Some of the walls have been painted in a forgiving soft white, whereas others are left unpainted with their clay plaster on display,

ABOVE The dark painting by Helsinki-based painter Johanna Aalto that dominates this wall breaks up the grey tones, which could otherwise feel a little oppressive. The enormous steel-framed sofa by Finnish company Adea, provides a more than generous perch for all the family. The deep blue of the upholstery anchors the sofa in the room and makes it the focal point – an important consideration for Ulla in her attempt to create a friendly family home. The central cushion is a long Hungarian grain sack. The low table, which holds an array of Ulla's collection of beautiful design books, was formerly less glamorously employed as a factory trolley.

ABOVE LEFT The long wooden floorboards stretch out along the floor and add to the sense of space as they lead towards the bathroom. The large windows that are integral to the overall design of the house flood the space with daylight.

ABOVE RIGHT In Ulla's workspace, a corner sofa, upholstered in a lovely deep Prussian blue linen, offers a spot to contemplate and dream while gazing out at the forest views. A bank of neatly-labelled files are testament to the huge array of projects that Ulla has worked on as designer and editor-in-chief of *Deko* interior design magazine and also in her work with Woodnotes, Durat, Artek and Marimekko.

in shadowy muted tones of grey. The colours used throughout the home, carefully chosen by Ulla, are a serene palette of white, grey, deep blue and ever so slightly off black. Their predominance ensures that nothing jars and there is a real sense of harmony.

Ulla was adamant that she wanted a large open-plan ground floor. This is a communal area where the whole family can get together on a daily basis, but there are also cosy corners, thanks to the inclusion of a few extra walls that break up the space but don't close it off entirely. These offer individuals the chance to go off and do their own thing when they feel the need. To fit the demands of the family there is an expansive squishy sofa, upholstered in Ulla's favourite shade of inky blue and piled with heaps of soft cushions. There are also large cushions scattered on the floor, some of which are the sculptural 'My' cushion designed by Ulla for Woodnotes and covered in cotton fabric made with paper yarn.

As a designer Ulla is well aware of the unique ability of the handmade to invest a home with personality. Her home is full of carefully chosen bespoke objects, which sit happily together thanks to the link of craftsmanship. Ulla's favourites include Ingo Maurer's Zettel'z

ABOVE A simple yet delicious lunch of soft, heart-shaped Neufchâtel French cheese and traditional dark Scandinavian rye bread is served on a roughly hewn long wooden chopping board, which in turn sits on an even more roughly textured wooden surface, awaiting the hungry hordes.

ABOVE Ulla has a huge collection of plates and bowls, many of them oriental in origin. The top shelf of this deep-set kitchen cupboard holds stacks of blue and white striped teacups, with the occasional more unusual yellow and white one just creeping into view. The wobbly edges of a stack of fluted plates on the shelf below are testament to the unique qualities of the handmade, with their fine lack of uniformity.

OPPOSITE The hard-working nuts and bolts of the kitchen are hidden away behind a roughly plastered wall. However, the long wooden breakfast bar protrudes from behind the wall into the living space, meaning that kitchen tasks can become more sociable.

chandelier, where the crystal drops are replaced by pieces of paper that can be unclipped and written on when the muse takes hold, making it a truly personal piece. More light is provided by the glowing blobs of Jasper Morrison's Glo-Ball pendant. Seating around the sleek, long dining table is provided by a team of mismatched designer chairs, including white Eames chairs and the simple lines of Maarten Van Severen's 0.3 chairs.

The kitchen is partially tucked away behind one of the half walls on the ground floor. On one side, the food preparation area extends to ensure that cooking is a social occasion, while at the other end there is a beautiful piece of bleached wood mounted on simple, almost scaffolding-like legs, peeking out into the living space, so Ulla can chat to the family while cooking. A tall bank of cupboards has been coated in a deep shade of kingfisher blue that contrasts

THIS PAGE A brightly coloured woollen blanket designed by Ulla lies in soft folds on a sturdy looking pouffe. This is a great portable perch for looking out into the forest through the generously sized floor-to-ceiling windows.

LEFT Simple white shelves hold evidence of a huge collection of books and magazines that Ulla just can't bear to throw away. Tins of paintbrushes and pens await a moment of inspiration, next to neatly stacked boxes and yet more books.

BELOW LEFT A bank of sleek white cupboards holds an array of unusual objects, including a pair of tiny handmade birds, ready to be illuminated by a clever little desk lamp. A group of ceramic vases with a vivid red glaze add colour to the collection, as does a large bright blue butterfly, mounted in a wood and glass frame.

BELOW This part of the house proves the range of Ulla's skills, with a sewing machine all threaded and ready to go, as well as a wooden model for figure drawing. The horizontal windows allow in plenty of light.

with the rough plastered walls behind. On top of these cupboards sits a row of wirework huts and houses that, from a distance, look like scribbles of black pen.

The restrained blue, white and grey colour palette continues on to the upper floor. Beds are draped with white bedspreads and there is a sculptural bedside lamp whose shape is reflected in the print of a long rectangular cushion. The dark blues of the room are restful. It is said that blue can lower blood pressure, so a good night's sleep is sure to be had in this house!

The bathroom is plain and simple, with a deep bath that is positioned to give bathers a view of the forest outside. The deliberate use of wood to support the similarly shaped sink and in the form of a primitive-looking stool relaxes the atmosphere in this room too, just as it does throughout the rest of the house.

RIGHT In the pared-down bathroom, a pile of towels is in keeping with the overall colour scheme of the house.

BELOW The back wall of the bedroom has been painted in a dark blue paint with a slightly metallic finish. It's reminiscent of the dark night skies in this part of the Finnish countryside, far away from the bright lights of the city. The deliberately crumpled-looking white bedspread was designed and handmade by Ulla.

OPPOSITE The bathroom offers an amazing view deep into the forest for anyone relaxing in the bath. There is no need to worry about privacy in this isolated spot. The deep, steep-sided angular bathtub and sink are made from Durat, a unique 100% recycled (and recyclable) composite material made from post-industrial plastics. Like so many of the beautiful things in this home, the bath and sink were designed by Ulla herself.

Q&A

What is your favourite thing about your home?
Space. The big, open space and the views through the rooms. And also the ever-changing view of the landscape.

What materials do you most like to work with?
I prefer materials that have strong character.

Do you prefer modern or vintage, and why?
Both. I like to mix things up and let the old and new have a conversation.

What is your favourite book?
I love books and we have plenty of them, so it's difficult to say – maybe *The Baron in the Trees* by Italo Calvino.

SOURCE DIRECTORY

UK

SHOPS AND ART SPACES

The Art Shop
8 Cross Street
Abergavenny
Monmouthshire
Wales NP7 5EH
www.artshopandgallery.co.uk
01873 852690
Art materials and books plus regular exhibitions of ceramics, paintings, prints and drawings.

Baileys
Whitecross Farm
Bridstow
Ross-on-Wye
Herefordshire HR9 6JU
01989 561931
www.baileyshome.com
Our store – a huge mix of new, vintage, recycled and, of course, the handmade.

Brook Street Pottery
Hay-on-Wye
Herefordshire HR3 5BQ
01497 821070
info@brookstreetpottery.co.uk
Contemporary terracotta and studio ceramics with regular exhibitions.

Caravan
www.caravanstyle.com
Emily Chalmers' quirky vintage style.

Le Chien et Moi
60 Derby Road
Nottingham NG1 5FD
0115 9799199
www.lechienetmoi.com
A diverse and considered collection of unusual and beautiful things for the home, both old and new and with a touch of nostalgia.

The Cloth House
47 & 98 Berwick Street
London W1F 8SJ
020 7437 5155
www.clothhouse.com
Fabrics from all over the world, many made by local craftspeople.

Contemporary Applied Arts
2 Percy Street
London W1T 1DD
020 7436 2344
www.caa.org.uk
The best of British craft. They also provide a commissioning service.

Contemporary Ceramics Centre
63 Great Russell Street
London WC1B 3BF
020 7242 9644
www.cpaceramics.com
Unique showcase for contemporary studio ceramics.

Damson & Slate
33 High Street
Narberth
Pembrokeshire SA67 7JE
01834 862877
www.damsonandslate.co.uk
Specializing in Welsh art and craft.

The End
Castle Street
Hay-on-Wye
Herefordshire
07779 788520
Hungarian linen and antiques.

England & Co
216 Westbourne Grove
London W11 2RH
020 7221 0417
www.englandgallery.com
Emerging and established contemporary artists.

Few and Far
242 Brompton Road
London SW3 2BB
020 7225 7070
www.fewandfar.net
A surprising mix of clothing collections from India, France and Morocco plus contemporary and vintage furniture, toys and craft.

Found
17 Argyle Street
Bath BA2 4BQ
01225 422001
www.foundbath.co.uk
Clothes, jewellery and homewares.

Frank
65 Harbour Street
Whitstable
Kent CT5 1AG
01227 262500
www.frankworks.eu
Handmade and homemade craft, decorative pieces and artworks.

Gallery Bailey
www.gallerybailey.com
Ceramics, paintings, sculpture and found objects.

The Gallery
Ruthin Craft Centre
Park Road
Ruthin
Denbighshire LL15 1BB
01824 704774
www.ruthincraftcentre.org.uk
A state-of-the-art craft centre with studios, workshop and three galleries.

Kettle's Yard
Castle Street
Cambridge CB3 0AQ
01223 748100
www.kettlesyard.co.uk
A distinctive collection of modern art.

Liberty
Regent Street
London W1B 5AH
020 7734 1234
www.liberty.co.uk
Iconic London department store where contemporary and craft sit happily side by side.

Le Magasin
50a Cliffe High Street
Lewes
East Sussex BN7 2AN
01273 474720
Café with vintage French furniture for sale. Great cakes, coffee and Curious Chocolate.

Material
131 Corve Street
Ludlow
Shropshire SY8 2PG
01584 877952
www.materialmaterial.com
Gallery and bookshop selling limited edition prints and beautiful books.

Melanie Giles Hairdressing
59 Walcot Street
Bath BA1 5BN
01225 444448
www.melanie-giles.co.uk
Haircuts in a handmade setting. New salon just opened in Frome.

Pigeon Vintage Furniture
1a Pelham Street
Brighton BN1 4FA
07930 357362
www.pigeonvintage.co.uk
Utility and industrial furniture and pieces designed with functionality and durability in mind.

Richard Booth's Bookshop
44 Lion Street
Hay-on-Wye
Herefordshire HR3 5AA
01497 820322
www.boothbooks.co.uk
Incredible book store and we like to eat in the café.

Robert Young
68 Battersea Bridge Road
London SW11 3AG
020 7228 7847
www.robertyoungantiques.com
Folk art, furniture and accessories.

St Jude's
Wolterton Road
Itteringham
Norfolk NR11 7AF
01263 587666
www.stjudesgallery.co.uk
Specializing in British printmaking, art, craft and design.

SCP
135–159 Curtain Road
London EC2A 3BX
020 7739 1869
www.scp.co.uk
Modern furniture and contemporary design.

Selvedge
162 Archway Road
London N6 5BB
020 8341 9721
www.selvedge.org
A bi-monthly magazine about contemporary art and crafts.

Summerill and Bishop
100 Portland Road
London W11 4LQ
020 7229 1337
www.summerillandbishop.com
Handcrafted earthenware, glassware and natural home products.

Swag
91 Trafalgar Street
Brighton BN1 4ER
01273 688504
www.swagantiques.com
Tarnished gilt mirrors and old shop fittings.

Unpackaged
42 Amwell Street
London EC1R 1XT
020 7713 8368
www.beunpackaged.com
Simple food shopping without all the unnecessary packaging – take your own containers.

Vessel
114 Kensington Park Road
London W11 2PW
020 7727 8001
www.vesselgallery.com
A modern Mecca for all those who appreciate good design.

Yew Tree Gallery
Keigwin Farmhouse
Nr Morvah
Pendeen
Cornwall TR19 7TS
01736 786425
www.yewtreegallery.com
Sculpture, jewellery and ceramics.

Yorkshire Sculpture Park
West Bretton
Wakefield WF4 4LG
01924 832631
www.ysp.co.uk
Contemporary arts and craft.

ANTIQUE AND FLEA MARKETS
There are many regular antique fairs around the country. For information, visit www.antiques-atlas.com.

MARKETS IN LONDON
Portobello
Portobello Road W11
Saturday, 8am to 5pm.
www.portobelloroad.co.uk

Brick Lane
Brick Lane, Cheshire Street
Sclater Street, E1 and E2
Sunday, 8am to 2pm
www.visitbricklane.org

Bermondsey
Bermondsey Square, SE1
Friday, 4am to 1pm

Camden
Camden High Street, NW1
Daily.
www.camdenlock.net

Greenwich
Greenwich Church Street
Stockwell Street,
Greenwick High Road, SE10
Wednesday–Sunday, 10am to 5.30pm.
www.greenwich-market.co.uk

PAINT
Auro Organic Paints
Cheltenham Road
Bisley
Nr Stroud
Gloucestershire, GL6 7BX
01452 772020
www.auro.co.uk
Natural emulsions, eggshells and chalk paints in muted colours. Also floor finishes and wood stains.

Clayworks
01326 341339
www.clay-works.com
Naturally beautiful pigmented clay plasters.

Earthborn Paints
Frodsham Business Centre
Bridge Lane
Frodsham
Cheshire WA6 7FZ
01928 734171
www.earthbornpaints.co.uk
Superior quality eco-paints that look sublime.

US

FURNITURE
BDDW
5 Crosby Street
New York, NY 10013
(+1) 212 625 1230
www.bddw.com
Handmade, timeless American furniture crafted from solid wood.

Bergen Office Furniture
127 West 26th Street
New York, NY 10001
(+1) 212 366 6677
www.bergenofficefurniture.com
Mid-century steel office furniture.

John Derian Dry Goods
10 East Second Street
New York, NY 10003
(+1) 212 677 8408
www.johnderian.com
Furniture upholstered in natural linen plus inspiring antiques, prints and home accessories.

White Trash
304 East 5th Street
New York, NY 10003
(+1) 212 598 5956
www.whitetrashnyc.com
Mid-century modern furnishings.

SALVAGE AND RECLAMATION
Olde Good Things
Union Square
5 East 16th Street
New York, NY 10003
(+1) 212 989 8814
www.ogtstore.com
Architectural salvage and altered antiques.

Historic Houseparts
540 South Avenue
Rochester, NY 14620
(+1) 585 325 2329
www.historichouseparts.com
Salvaged doors, sinks, and tiles.

Sylvan Brandt
756 Rothsville Road
Lititz, PA 17543
(+1) 717 626 4520
www.sylvanbrandt.com
Reclaimed and weatherboard flooring, beams, and architectural antiques.

PAINT
Earth Pigments
(+1) 520 682-8928
www.earthpigments.com
Non-toxic pigments for tinting lime or clay plaster or concrete.

Farrow & Ball
112 Mercer Street
New York, NY 10012
(+1) 212 334 8330
www.farrow-ball.com
Quality paint colours.

The Old Fashioned Milk Paint Co.
436 Main Street
Groton, MA 01450
(+1) 866 350-6455
www.milkpaint.com
Environmentally safe, non-toxic milk paint in historical colours.

TEXTILES
De Le Cuona
D & D Building, Suite 914
979 Third Avenue
New York, NY 10022
(+1) 212 702 0800
www.delecuona.co.uk
Linens in a choice of muted or neutral colours.

O Eco Textiles
942 18th Avenue East
Seattle, WA 98112
(+1) 206 633 1177
www.oecotextiles.com
Eco textiles including linen and hemp upholstery fabric.

ART AND ACCESSORIES
Ted Muehling
57 Walker Street
New York, NY 10013
(+1) 212 431 3825
www.tedmuehling.com
Objects and jewellery,

Ochre
462 Broome Street
New York, NY 10013
(+1) 212 414 4332
www.ochrestore.com
Vintage and organic textiles, ceramics, glassware and baskets.

Michele Varian
27 Howard Street
New York, NY 10013
(+1) 212 226 1076
www.michelevarian.com
Industrial-style furniture, lighting and ceramics.

BUSINESS CREDITS

The Art Shop and Gallery
8 Cross Street
Abergavenny
Monmouthshire
Wales NP7 5EH
www.artshopandgallery.co.uk
01873 852690
*Pages 8; 14; 32 right; 33; 46 below;
52; 60 centre–63.*

Baileys
Whitecross Farm
Bridstow
Ross-on-Wye
Herefordshire HR9 6JU
01989 561931
www.baileyshome.com
*Pages 16 below left; 17; 21 above
right; 22 centre; 43; 49 below; 51;
54 below; 55; 57 above right; 57
below right; 58 above left; 64–71.*

Gallery Bailey
www.gallerybailey.com
*10–13; 16 above left; 19; 21 above
left; 30; 32 centre; 39 above right;
44; 46 above; 48 left; 49 above
right; 54 above left; 56; 57 above
left; 78–87; 160.*

Kate Blee
E:kate@kateblee.co.uk
www.kateblee.co.uk
*Pages 19 below left; 22 right; 31;
40–41; 57 below left; 88–95.*

Bryn Eglur
Bryn Eglur is available to rent at
www.thewelshhouse.co.uk
*Pages 18 above; 20; 29 above
right and below right; 49 above
left; 96–103.*

Bryncyn
Bryncyn is available to rent at
www.thewelshhouse.co.uk
*Front endpapers; 24; 26 left; 29
above left; 48 right; 120–127.*

Few and Far
242 Brompton Road
London SW3 2BB
+44 (0)20 7225 7070
E: shop@fewandfar.net
www.fewandfar.net
Pages 4; 29 below left; 72–77.

ina & matt
Studio INA-MATT
Riegeweg 14
8749 TD Pingjum
The Netherlands
E: info@ina-matt.com
+ 31 517 579 717
www.ina-matt.com
Pages 5; 22 left; 38; 58–59; 112–119.

Arie & Ingrams Design
Old Hall Barn
Penhill Road
Great Ellingham
Norfolk NR17 1LR
01953 4555556
E: info@arieandingramsdesign.com
www.arieandingramsdesign.com
Paintings by Fred Ingrams
www.fredingrams.com
*Pages 16 above right; 36 below; 37;
54 above right; 59 right; 138–145.*

Studio Claudy Jongstra
E: info@claudyjongstra.com
www.claudyjongstra.com
*Pages 21 below right; 23; 26 right;
27; 32; 42; 104–111.*

Ulla Koskinen & Sameli Rantanen
E: koskinen.rantanen@sci.fi
*Pages 2–3; 34; 36 above right;
146–155.*

Leslie Oschmann
Swarm
www.swarmhome.com
*Pages 1; 6; 9; 18 below right; 47;
50; 60 left; back endpapers.*

Fog Linen Work
5-35-1 Daita Setagaya
Tokyo
Japan 155-0033
+81 3 5432 5610
E: info@foglinenwork.com
www.foglinenwork.com
http://www.foglinenwork.com
for stockists worldwide
*Pages 36 above left; 39 below right;
132–137.*

PICTURE CREDITS

All photography by Debi Treloar
Front endpaper: Bryncyn is available for
holiday rental at www.thewelshhouse.org;
1 The home of the designer Leslie
Oschmann in Amsterdam; 2–3 The family
home of designers Ulla Koskinen &
Sameli Rantanen in Finland; 4 The home
in Hampshire of Priscilla Carluccio
shopkeeper and owner of Few and Far,
Brompton Road, London; 5 The home
and studio of the Dutch architects Ina &
Matt www.ina-matt.com; 6 The home of
the designer Leslie Oschmann in
Amsterdam; 8 Pauline Griffiths, owner of
The Art Shop and Gallery, Abergavenny;
9 The home of the designer Leslie
Oschmann in Amsterdam; 10–13
www.gallerybailey.com; 14 Pauline
Griffiths, owner of The Art Shop and
Gallery, Abergavenny; 16 above & below
left www.baileyshome.com; 16 above
right The family home in Norfolk of Laura
& Fred Ingrams of Arie & Ingrams Design;
17 www.baileyshome.com; 18 above
Bryn Eglur is available for holiday rental
at www.thewelshhouse.org; 19 below left
The family home and studio of artist Kate
Blee and architect Charles Thomson;
18 below right The home of the designer
Leslie Oschmann in Amsterdam; 19
www.gallerybailey.com; 20 Bryn Eglur is
available for holiday rental at
www.thewelshhouse.org; 21 above left
www.gallerybailey.com; 21 above right
www.baileyshome.com; 21 below right
The home of the artist Claudy Jongstra in
the Netherlands; 22 left The home and
studio of Dutch architects Ina & Matt
www.ina-matt.com; 22 centre
www.baileyshome.com; 22 right The
family home and studio of artist Kate Blee
and architect Charles Thomson; 23 The
home of the artist Claudy Jongstra in the
Netherlands; 24 Bryncyn is available for
holiday rental at www.thewelshhouse.org;
26 left Bryncyn is available for holiday
rental at www.thewelshhouse.org; 26
right and 27 The home of the artist
Claudy Jongstra in the Netherlands; 28
Yuko Wanatabe; 29 above left 24 Bryncyn
is available for holiday rental at
www.thewelshhouse.org; 29 above right
and below right Bryn Eglur is available for
holiday rental at www.thewelshhouse.org;
29 below left The home in Hampshire of
Priscilla Carluccio shopkeeper and owner
of Few and Far, Brompton Road, London;
30 www.gallerybailey.com; 31 The family
home and studio of artist Kate Blee and
architect Charles Thomson; 32 left The
home of the artist Claudy Jongstra in the
Netherlands; 32 centre
www.gallerybailey.com; 32 right and 33
Pauline Griffiths, owner of The Art Shop
and Gallery, Abergavenny; 34 The family
home of designers Ulla Koskinen &
Sameli Rantanen in Finland; 36 above left
The home of Yumiko Sekine of
www.foglinenwork.com; 36 above right
The family home of designers Ulla
Koskinen & Sameli Rantanen in Finland;

36 below and 37 The family home in
Norfolk of Laura & Fred Ingrams of Arie
& Ingrams Design; 38 The home and
studio of Dutch architects Ina & Matt
www.ina-matt.com; 39 above left Yuko;
39 above right www.gallerybailey.com; 39
below right The home of Yumiko Sekine
of www.foglinenwork.com; 40–41 The
family home and studio of artist Kate Blee
and architect Charles Thomson; 42 The
home of the artist Claudy Jongstra in the
Netherlands; 43 www.baileyshome.com;
44 www.gallerybailey.com; 46 above
www.gallerybailey.com; 46 below Pauline
Griffiths, owner of The Art Shop and
Gallery, Abergavenny; 47 The home
of the designer Leslie Oschmann in
Amsterdam; 48 left www.gallerybailey.com;
48 right Bryncyn is available for holiday
rental at www.thewelshhouse.org; 49
above left Bryn Eglur is available for
holiday rental at www.thewelshhouse.org;
49 above right www.gallerybailey.com;
49 below www.baileyshome.com; 50 The
home of the designer Leslie Oschmann in
Amsterdam; 51 www.baileyshome.com;
52 Pauline Griffiths, owner of The Art
Shop and Gallery, Abergavenny; 54
above left www.gallerybailey.com; 54
above right The family home in Norfolk
of Laura & Fred Ingrams of Arie &
Ingrams Design; 54 below and 55
www.baileyshome.com; 56 and 57 above
left www.gallerybailey.com; 57 above
right www.baileyshome.com; 57 below
left The family home and studio of artist
Kate Blee and architect Charles
Thomson; 57 below right and 58 above
left www.baileyshome.com; 58–59 The
home and studio of the Dutch architects
Ina & Matt www.ina-matt.com; 59 right
The family home in Norfolk of Laura &
Fred Ingrams of Arie & Ingrams Design;
60 left The home of the designer Leslie
Oschmann in Amsterdam; 60 centre–63
Pauline Griffiths, owner of The Art Shop
and Gallery, Abergavenny; 64–71
www.baileyshome.com; 72–77 The home
in Hampshire of Priscilla Carluccio
shopkeeper and owner of Few and Far,
Brompton Road, London; 78–87
www.gallerybailey.com; 88–95 The family
home and studio of artist Kate Blee and
architect Charles Thomson; 96–103 Bryn
Eglur is available for holiday rental at
www.thewelshhouse.org; 104–111 The
home of the artist Claudy Jongstra in the
Netherlands; 112–119 The home and
studio of the Dutch architects Ina & Matt
www.ina-matt.com; 120–127 Bryncyn is
available for holiday rental at
www.thewelshhouse.org; 128–131 Yuko
Watanabe; 132–137 The home of Yumiko
Sekine of www.foglinenwork.com; 138–
145 The family home in Norfolk of Laura
& Fred Ingrams of Arie & Ingrams Design;
146–155 The family home of designers
Ulla Koskinen & Sameli Rantanen in
Finland; 160 www.gallerybailey.com; back
endpaper: The home of the designer
Leslie Oschmann in Amsterdam.

INDEX

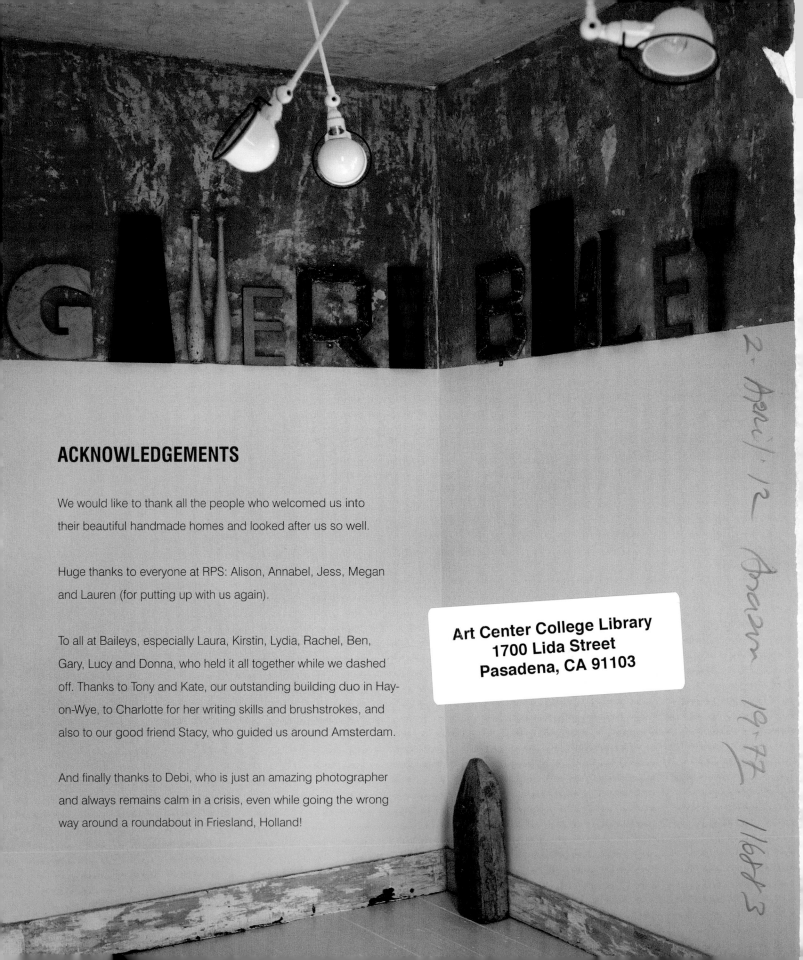

ACKNOWLEDGEMENTS

We would like to thank all the people who welcomed us into their beautiful handmade homes and looked after us so well.

Huge thanks to everyone at RPS: Alison, Annabel, Jess, Megan and Lauren (for putting up with us again).

To all at Baileys, especially Laura, Kirstin, Lydia, Rachel, Ben, Gary, Lucy and Donna, who held it all together while we dashed off. Thanks to Tony and Kate, our outstanding building duo in Hay-on-Wye, to Charlotte for her writing skills and brushstrokes, and also to our good friend Stacy, who guided us around Amsterdam.

And finally thanks to Debi, who is just an amazing photographer and always remains calm in a crisis, even while going the wrong way around a roundabout in Friesland, Holland!